D0001134

OPPOSING VIEWPOINTS® SERIES

Domestic Violence

Other Books of Related Interest:

Opposing Viewpoints Series

Violence

Sexual Violence

Current Controversies Series

Violence Against Women

At Issue Series

Date Rape

"Congress shall make no law . . . abridging the freedom of speech, or of the press."

First Amendment to the U.S. Constitution

The basic foundation of our democracy is the First Amendment guarantee of freedom of expression. The *Opposing Viewpoints* Series is dedicated to the concept of this basic freedom and the idea that it is more important to practice it than to enshrine it.

OPPOSING VIEWPOINTS® SERIES

Domestic Violence

Mike Wilson, Book Editor

GREENHAVEN PRESS
A part of Gale, Cengage Learning

GALE
CENGAGE Learning™

Detroit • New York • San Francisco • New Haven, Conn • Waterville, Maine • London

Christine Nasso, *Publisher*
Elizabeth Des Chenes, *Managing Editor*

© 2009 Greenhaven Press, a part of Gale, Cengage Learning

Gale and Greenhaven Press are registered trademarks used herein under license.

For more information, contact:
Greenhaven Press
27500 Drake Rd.
Farmington Hills, MI 48331-3535
Or you can visit our Internet site at gale.cengage.com

For product information and technology assistance, contact us at

Gale Customer Support, 1-800-877-4253
For permission to use material from this text or product, submit all requests online at www.cengage.com/permissions

Further permissions questions can be emailed to permissionrequest@cengage.com

Articles in Greenhaven Press anthologies are often edited for length to meet page requirements. In addition, original titles of these works are changed to clearly present the main thesis and to explicitly indicate the author's opinion. Every effort is made to ensure that Greenhaven Press accurately reflects the original intent of the authors. Every effort has been made to trace the owners of copyrighted material.

Cover image © iStock.

LIBRARY OF CONGRESS CATALOGING-IN-PUBLICATION DATA

Domestic violence / Mike Wilson, book editor.
    p. cm. -- (Opposing viewpoints)
    Includes bibliographical references and index.
    ISBN-13: 978-0-7377-4206-0 (hardcover)
    ISBN-13: 978-0-7377-4207-7 (pbk.)
    1. Family violence. 2. Family violence--Prevention. I. Wilson, Mike, 1954-
    HV6626.D634 2009
    362.82'92--dc22

                                     2008028517

Printed in the United States of America
1 2 3 4 5 6 7 12 11 10 09 08

Contents

Chapter 2: Who Is Responsible for Domestic Violence?

Chapter 3: Is the Law Effective in Dealing with Domestic Violence?

Why Consider Opposing Viewpoints?

> *"The only way in which a human being can make some approach to knowing the whole of a subject is by hearing what can be said about it by persons of every variety of opinion and studying all modes in which it can be looked at by every character of mind. No wise man ever acquired his wisdom in any mode but this."*
>
> *John Stuart Mill*

In our media-intensive culture it is not difficult to find differing opinions. Thousands of newspapers and magazines and dozens of radio and television talk shows resound with differing points of view. The difficulty lies in deciding which opinion to agree with and which "experts" seem the most credible. The more inundated we become with differing opinions and claims, the more essential it is to hone critical reading and thinking skills to evaluate these ideas. *Opposing Viewpoints* books address this problem directly by presenting stimulating debates that can be used to enhance and teach these skills. The varied opinions contained in each book examine many different aspects of a single issue. While examining these conveniently edited opposing views, readers can develop critical thinking skills such as the ability to compare and contrast authors' credibility, facts, argumentation styles, use of persuasive techniques, and other stylistic tools. In short, the *Opposing Viewpoints* series is an ideal way to attain the higher-level thinking and reading skills so essential in a culture of diverse and contradictory opinions.

In addition to providing a tool for critical thinking, *Opposing Viewpoints* books challenge readers to question their own strongly held opinions and assumptions. Most people form their opinions on the basis of upbringing, peer pressure, and personal, cultural, or professional bias. By reading carefully balanced opposing views, readers must directly confront new ideas as well as the opinions of those with whom they disagree. This is not to simplistically argue that everyone who reads opposing views will—or should—change his or her opinion. Instead, the series enhances readers' understanding of their own views by encouraging confrontation with opposing ideas. Careful examination of others' views can lead to the readers' understanding of the logical inconsistencies in their own opinions, perspective on why they hold an opinion, and the consideration of the possibility that their opinion requires further evaluation.

Evaluating Other Opinions

To ensure that this type of examination occurs, *Opposing Viewpoints* books present all types of opinions. Prominent spokespeople on different sides of each issue as well as well-known professionals from many disciplines challenge the reader. An additional goal of the series is to provide a forum for other, less known, or even unpopular viewpoints. The opinion of an ordinary person who has had to make the decision to cut off life support from a terminally ill relative, for example, may be just as valuable and provide just as much insight as a medical ethicist's professional opinion. The editors have two additional purposes in including these less known views. One, the editors encourage readers to respect others' opinions—even when not enhanced by professional credibility. It is only by reading or listening to and objectively evaluating others' ideas that one can determine whether they are worthy of consideration. Two, the inclusion of such viewpoints encourages the important critical thinking skill of objectively evaluating an author's credentials and bias. This evaluation will illuminate an author's reasons for taking a particular stance on an issue and will aid in readers' evaluation of the author's ideas.

It is our hope that these books will give readers a deeper understanding of the issues debated and an appreciation of the complexity of even seemingly simple issues when good and honest people disagree. This awareness is particularly important in a democratic society such as ours in which people enter into public debate to determine the common good. Those with whom one disagrees should not be regarded as enemies but rather as people whose views deserve careful examination and may shed light on one's own.

Thomas Jefferson once said that "difference of opinion leads to inquiry, and inquiry to truth." Jefferson, a broadly educated man, argued that "if a nation expects to be ignorant and free. . .it expects what never was and never will be." As individuals and as a nation, it is imperative that we consider the opinions of others and examine them with skill and discernment. The *Opposing Viewpoints* series is intended to help readers achieve this goal.

David L. Bender and Bruno Leone,
Founders

Introduction

"Families are indispensable to a stable society, and they should be a place of support to instill responsibility and values in the next generation. When a family member is abused, it can have long-term damaging effects on the victim that leave a mark on family, friends, and the community at large." —George W. Bush, forty-third president of the United States, October 2007, proclaiming October as National Domestic Violence Awareness Month

Domestic violence is evident in the earliest records of human civilization. While both men and women are victims of domestic violence, according to the American Medical Association, women are more likely to experience physical injuries and incur the psychological consequences of domestic abuse than other family members. And although there are other types of domestic violence—sibling against sibling or caretaker against elderly patient, for example—until recent decades, the social and political context for domestic violence has been the authority of men over women.

In ancient Rome, wives were subject to chastisement by husbands. European Christendom in the Middle Ages also approved chastisement. Friar Cherubino of Siena, writing in the fifteenth century in *Rules of Marriage*, advised husbands to beat their wives when necessary. Cherubino offered the following advice to husbands regarding their wives: "Scold her sharply, bully and terrify her. And if that still doesn't work, take up a stick and beat her soundly. Not in rage but out of charity and concern for her soul, so the beating will resound to your merit."

Reva B. Siegel, writing in the *Yale Law Journal*, notes that "Anglo-American common law originally provided that a husband, as master of his household, could subject his wife to corporal punishment or 'chastisement' so long as he did not inflict permanent injury upon her."

During the latter part of the nineteenth century, an era of feminist agitation for reform of marriage law, authorities in England and the United States began declaring that a husband no longer had the right to chastise his wife. The 1871 case of *Fulgham v. State* in Alabama ruled that "the wife is not to be considered as the husband's slave. And the privilege, ancient though it be, to beat her with a stick, to pull her hair, choke her, spit in her face or kick her about the floor, or to inflict upon her like indignities, is not now acknowledged by our law."

However, Siegel points out that even though courts were repudiating the husband's right to chastise his wife, the legal system still treated wife-beating differently from other cases of assault and battery. Siegel says that "while authorities denied that a husband had the right to beat his wife, they intervened only intermittently in cases of marital violence." The different treatment, according to Siegel, was rationalized as necessary "in order to protect the privacy of the family and to promote 'domestic harmony.'"

Women obtained the right to vote in America and England in the early part of the twentieth century, but it was not until the women's movement in the late 1960s and early 1970s that public consciousness began to focus on the problem of domestic violence. Publication in 1974 of the book *Scream Quietly or the Neighbors Will Hear,* by Erin Pizzey, presented domestic violence from the perspective of the victim, which had a significant effect on the public's awareness of the problem. In addition to her work as an author, Pizzey founded the first shelter for battered women in the twentieth century, which was set up in England. Such shelters spread throughout

England and became models for shelters and safe houses established in America and elsewhere by women's groups.

During the 1980s, domestic violence was becoming a social and legal issue, rather than a private family matter. In 1980, a pilot program by The Domestic Abuse Intervention Project in the city of Duluth, Minnesota, combined the efforts of police, prosecutors, courts, social workers, battered women's shelters, and others to address the issue of domestic violence. The "Duluth Model," as it came to be known, evolved into a program that was subsequently adopted by many other cities.

Domestic violence began to take a more prominent place in the political and legislative agenda of the nation during the 1980s and 1990s. The Task Force on Family Violence was established by the U.S. attorney general's office in 1983. A National Institute of Justice and Police Foundation study in Minneapolis in 1984 found that arrest was more effective in reducing repeat domestic violence offenses than not arresting perpetrators. In 1985, U.S. surgeon general C. Everett Koop named domestic violence "a public health menace that police alone cannot cope with."

In 1990, the Violence Against Women Act (VAWA) was introduced by then-U.S. congresswoman (now senator) Barbara Boxer of California. VAWA attempted to hold perpetrators of domestic violence accountable and provide protections to women. VAWA did not pass during the first attempt but was finally signed into law on September 13, 1994, and since then has been reauthorized several times.

In time, a men's rights movement critical of VAWA appeared. Men claimed domestic violence incidence was exaggerated, that allegations often were false and made to gain an advantage in divorce or custody litigation, and that domestic violence proceedings were unfair to men. In the view of psychology professor Gordon E. Finley, domestic violence programs are "predicated on the false presumption men always are the predatory perpetrators and women always the innocent victims," though much research shows that men and women initiate domestic violence at nearly equal rates.

Many of those critical of VAWA claim that domestic violence laws encourage the breakup of the family and the isolation of men from their wives and children, rather than attempting to keep the family together. Because women are awarded custody in a divorce more often than men are, some fathers feel that laws like VAWA destroy their families and wrongfully separate them from their children.

It is not only intimate partners who experience the consequences of domestic violence. The National Center for Victims of Crime (NCVC) states that "domestic violence affects not only those abused, but witnesses, family members, coworkers, friends, and the community at large." NCVC points out that children who witness domestic violence are victims themselves, and growing up amidst violence predisposes them to a multitude of social and physical problems. According to NCVC, "Constant exposure to violence in the home and abusive role models teaches these children that violence is a normal way of life and places them at risk of becoming society's next generation of victims and abusers."

Domestic violence affects the workplace as well. The American Institute on Domestic Violence (AIDV) says victims of intimate partner violence lose nearly 8 million days of paid work each year—the equivalent of thirty-two thousand full-time jobs. AIDV notes that domestic violence is the leading cause of death for women in the workplace and that approximately 18,700 incidents of domestic violence are committed in the U.S. workplace each year by a victim's current or former spouse, lover, partner, or boyfriend/girlfriend.

Law professor Linda Kelly, writing in the *Florida State University Law Review*, has noted that domestic violence "represents the prized gemstone of feminist theory's fundamental message that our legal, social and cultural norms are fashioned in a manner which permit men to engage in a constant and pervasive effort to oppress women by any and every available means."

However, the fact that significant domestic violence is perpetrated by women against men calls into question whether patriarchy alone can explain the cause of all domestic violence. After all, domestic violence occurs between gay and lesbian intimate partners and between siblings as well.

When it comes to deducing the causes of domestic violence, it is difficult to find a "one size fits all" explanation. In *Opposing Viewpoints: Domestic Violence*, the contributors discuss domestic violence in the following chapters: Is Domestic Violence a Serious Problem? Who Is Responsible for Domestic Violence? Is the Law Effective in Dealing with Domestic Violence? and How Can Domestic Violence Be Prevented? The authors aim to deconstruct this subject that touches so many individuals and to seek solutions to the complex problem of domestic violence.

OPPOSING
VIEWPOINTS®
SERIES

CHAPTER 1

Is Domestic Violence a Serious Problem?

Chapter Preface

According to the Family Violence Prevention Fund, "Studies suggest that between 3.3 and 10 million children are exposed to domestic violence annually." In more than half of these situations, spousal abuse has led to the abuse of children. Children exposed to family violence face not only an assault to their physical being but also mental and emotional abuse, as well as other unique challenges.

In *Ending the Cycle of Violence: Community Responses to Children of Battered Women*, the authors have drawn a correlation between children from abusive families and behavioral issues, such as increased aggression toward peers. In addition, they found that children from these disturbed households were more likely to use illegal drugs and to commit crimes later in life, such as sexual assault.

The Family Violence Prevention Fund also reports that "one study of 2,245 children and teenagers found that recent exposure to violence in the home was a significant factor in predicting a child's violent behavior." This aggression led to higher rates of expulsion and often eliminated or severely restricted career and educational opportunities.

Along with increased aggression, researchers have found that domestic violence impacts a child's mental and physical well-being. Studies have shown that children from these families have increased rates of depression and attempt suicide more often than those from stable families. One 2005 study from the *Journal of Pediatrics* found that "children who had been exposed to violence suffered symptoms of post-traumatic stress disorder, such as bed-wetting or nightmares, and were at a greater risk than their peers of having allergies, asthma, gastrointestinal problems, headaches and flu." Based on this and similar studies, an unstable home environment may lead to an increase in a variety of mental and physical ailments.

The challenges that domestic violence poses for children may continue to affect them—even into adulthood—until those issues are addressed. Indeed, studies have shown that men who are exposed to domestic violence as children are more apt to abuse their own children and spouses, setting up a cycle of abuse that is often difficult to break. In addition to the short-term challenges, this long-term cycle makes identifying and addressing abuse a top priority for children's rights groups throughout the world.

The following chapter poses the question of whether domestic violence is a serious problem. The authors take unique perspectives on the nature of the problem and the groups that are most at risk.

> *"There is a widespread belief that the ... United States did not begin to address ... domestic violence until quite recently. In fact, the very first laws in colonial-era America forbade wifebeating."*

Domestic Violence Has Been a Problem Throughout U.S. History

Cathy Young

In the following viewpoint, Cathy Young traces the evolution of the legislative and judicial response to domestic violence. She notes that penalties for spousal abuse were written into law as early as colonial times and continued to evolve into the nineteenth century. The rise of feminism in the 1960s and 1970s brought more attention to the problem, and by the late 1980s these types of abuses, which had come to be known as "family" assaults, were treated with the same seriousness as nonfamily crimes, Young asserts. The author concludes that while current measurements can be difficult to interpret, it is clear that domestic violence remains a serious problem.

Cathy Young, "Domestic Violence: An In-Depth Analysis," Independent Women's Forum Position Paper, September 2005. Reproduced with permission by Independent Women's Forum. www.iwf.org.

As you read, consider the following questions:

1. What was the primary function of the police in domestic disputes in the 1960s and 1970s, according to Young?

2. What 1994 celebrity murder case dramatically raised public awareness of domestic abuse, as cited by the author?

3. Why is it difficult to measure the prevalence of domestic violence, in Young's opinion?

There is a widespread belief that the justice system in the United States did not begin to address the problem of domestic violence until quite recently. In fact, the very first laws in colonial-era America forbade wifebeating. The "Body of Liberties" adopted by the Massachusetts Bay colonists in 1641 stated, "Every married woman shall be free from bodily correction or stripes by her husband, unless it be in his own defense upon her assault." Wife-beaters could be punished with fines or whipping, and could also be subjected to public "shaming" in church or expelled from the congregation.

Nineteenth-Century Laws

Much attention has been drawn to the fact that in the 19th century, rulings by two appellate courts in the U.S., one in Mississippi and two in North Carolina (the last of them in 1868), held that a husband was allowed to use force toward his wife "in moderation." However, even the judges who issued those opinions recognized that they were outside the mainstream of judicial opinion for their time, and by the mid-1870s these courts also agreed that "the husband has no right to chastise his wife." However, the judges still expressed a preference for non-intervention when "no permanent injury has been inflicted, nor malice, cruelty nor dangerous violence shown by the husband." The feminist historian Elizabeth Pleck found in her research that 19th-century municipal courts "invariably accepted a woman's claim of physical abuse and took some action," which could range from a reprimand to a stay in jail to monetary compensation for the victim. While there were no specific domestic violence laws, domestic assaults could be and were prosecuted under assault and battery statutes. At the turn of the century, state legislation in Maryland, Delaware, and Oregon introduced flogging as a penalty for wife abusers. A similar federal law was considered by the U.S. Congress (though ultimately rejected) in 1906—nearly nine decades before the passage of the first federal law dealing with domestic violence, the Violence Against Women Act. . . .

Ironically, in the 1960s and 1970s, it was considered "progressive" to treat domestic violence as a family problem rather than a criminal matter; at the time, coercive law enforcements in general were unpopular and many offenses against the public order were decriminalized. Thus, a 1967 police manual said that "in dealing with family disputes, the power of arrest should be exercised only as a last resort." The American Bar Association took this position as well; its 1973 guidelines recommended that at least in urban areas, "the resolution of conflict such as that which occurs between husband and wife" should be conducted by the police "without reliance upon criminal assault or disorderly conduct statutes." Conflict mediation was regarded as the primary police function in what was then called domestic disputes.

Changing Attitudes

Only a few years later, however, the rise of feminism and the battered women's movement began to change prevailing attitudes toward domestic violence. The publication of landmark books such as *Battered Wives* by Del Martin drew attention to the plight of women in abusive marriages. The first large-scale studies on family violence, such as the 1975 National Family Violence Survey conducted by psychologists Murray A. Straus of the University of New Hampshire and Richard Gelles of the University of Rhode Island, found that battering was not just a matter of a few drunken bums beating up their wives or girlfriends but a fairly widespread problem, occurring in as many as 16 percent of American families every year. Straus and Gelles reported that two million women every year were battered by their spouses or partners, or experienced "severe" violence (defined as anything more violent than pushing, grabbing, or slapping—anything from punching or kicking to hitting with an object, choking, or using a weapon). While the surveys found an equally high rate of spousal violence by women, these findings did not elicit similar concern; female violence toward men was generally seen as far less dangerous and was commonly presumed to involve self-defense.

In the 1970s, the first shelters and crisis hotlines for battered women opened in the United States. Around the same time, there was a shift toward a more law enforcement–oriented approach to domestic violence. As commentator Cara Feinberg wrote in *The American Prospect*, "feminist activists began to see the law not only as an important tool for protecting victims but as a way to define domestic violence as a legitimate social problem." Several class-action lawsuits were filed challenging the failure of police to protect victims of domestic violence. In 1984, the case of Tracey Thurman, a Connecticut woman who filed a lawsuit after the police failed to intervene while she was repeatedly stabbed by her husband, reached the U.S. Supreme Court; Thurman won $2.3 million in compensatory damages. This award served as a wake-up call for many jurisdictions. . . .

Historically, legal protection for domestic violence victims in the United States has been uneven, varying greatly from place to place and from period to period. However, the best available research suggests that by the late 1980s men who assaulted their wives and girlfriends were not treated any more leniently than perpetrators in non-family assaults.

Kathleen Ferraro, a women's studies and criminology professor at Arizona State University who identifies herself as a

The Deep Impact of Violence Against Women

Violence against women has a far deeper impact than the immediate harm caused. It has devastating consequences for the women who experience it, and a traumatic effect on those who witness it, particularly children. It shames states that fail to prevent it and societies that tolerate it. Violence against women is a violation of basic human rights that must be eliminated through political will, and by legal and civil action in all sectors of society.

World Health Organization,
"WHO Multi-Country Study on Women's Health and
Domestic Violence Against Women," 2005. www.who.int.

"scholar/activist/survivor of male violence," analyzed the handling of violent offenses in Maricopa County, Arizona in 1987–88, expecting to find preferential treatment for batterers. However, she actually discovered that most assaults of any kind were either not prosecuted or prosecuted as misdemeanors. Among felony cases, domestic assaults were less likely to be dismissed than nondomestic ones. Only 11 percent of the defendants received any prison time at all, but the victim-offender relationship had no effect on the length of the sentence. An earlier study in Ohio came to a similar conclusion.

Nonetheless, concerns about the level of domestic violence and the still-inadequate and uncoordinated response to the problem led to a push for federal legislation to address violence against women. In 1994, the murders of Nicole Brown Simpson and Ron Goldman, and the arrest of retired celebrity athlete and convicted wife abuser O.J. Simpson on murder charges, dramatically raised public awareness of domestic abuse. That year, Congress passed the Violence Against Women

Act as part of an omnibus crime bill. VAWA was reauthorized and expanded in 2000. Meanwhile, both in response to VAWA and on their own initiative, most states and many jurisdictions across the U.S. strengthened their domestic violence legislation.

Current State of Affairs

Whether these efforts are paying off is often difficult to determine, since studies on the prevalence of domestic violence are often complicated by different definitions and measurements. According to data from the Bureau of Justice Statistics, the rate of non-fatal intimate violence in the United States dropped by nearly half between 1993 and 2001. The rates of domestic murders, too, have declined, though for some demographic groups such as African-American women the rates of murder victimization by intimates have stabilized in recent years after dropping sharply in the late 1970s and 1980s.

Domestic violence remains a serious and tragic problem. In recent years, there has been some debate about its true scope and prevalence. Some critics have accused anti-domestic violence activists of using inflated figures and drastically overstating the problem; in turn, many feminists have accused these critics of colluding in a backlash against battered women. There is no doubt that some widely used statistics—e.g. claims that battering causes more injuries to women than automobile accidents, rapes, and muggings combined, or that up to a 35 percent of women's emergency room visits are due to domestic violence—are false (data from the Centers for Disease Control and the Bureau of Justice Statistics suggest that the real figure is less than 2 percent). Nonetheless, the fact remains that serious, ongoing physical violence is estimated to exist in 2–3 percent of marriages in the United States. Every year, about 1,200 women and 500 men in this country die at the hand of a spouse or partner, and some 200,000 women and 40,000 men seek emergency room help due to domestic violence. Critiques of inflated statistics are entirely appropriate, but they should never be used to minimize or trivialize the real issue.

> *"Half [of all issued restraining orders] do not include any allegation of violence but rely on vague complaints made without evidence."*

The Incidence of Domestic Violence Is Exaggerated

Phyllis Schlafly

In the following viewpoint, Phyllis Schlafly argues that feminists and family court justices have exaggerated the incidence of domestic violence by expanding the definition of what constitutes such a crime. Hurt feelings and accusations, rather than overt acts, she says, are enough to result in findings of domestic violence under vaguely worded laws. Schlafly maintains that activist judges use such laws to criminalize otherwise legal behavior. Those accused are not, she asserts, entitled to presumption of innocence, proper standards of proof, and other rights normally part of due process in courts. Phyllis Schlafly is a well-known conservative political activist and the author of a number of books, including The Supremacists: The Tyranny of Judges and How to Stop It.

Phyllis Schlafly, "Feminists Responsible for Boom in Unnecessary Temporary Restraining Orders," humanevents.com, September 11, 2006. Reproduced by permission.

As you read, consider the following questions:

1. As an illustration of the excesses of domestic violence bureaucracy, Schlafly cites a restraining order issued against what television talk show host?

2. According to the author, how many domestic violence restraining orders are issued by family court judges each year?

3. Schlafly argues that women have an incentive to make false or exaggerated allegations of domestic violence in order to achieve what legal goals?

It brought to mind the title of the George Gershwin song "They All Laughed" when a Santa Fe, N.M., family court judge granted a temporary restraining order against "Late Show" host David Letterman to protect a woman he had never met, never heard of, and lived 2,000 miles away from.

Colleen Nestler claimed that Letterman had caused her "mental cruelty" and "sleep deprivation" for over a decade by using code words and gestures during his network television broadcasts.

That ridiculous temporary restraining order was dismissed in December [2005], but according to a report by Respecting Accuracy in Domestic Abuse Reporting, or RADAR, the case was not a judicial anomaly but "the logical culmination of years of ever-expanding definitions of domestic violence." RADAR is a Maryland-based think tank that specializes in exposing the excesses of the domestic violence bureaucracy.

Vague Definitions

The New Mexico statute defines domestic violence as causing "severe emotional distress." That definition was met when Nestler claimed she suffered from exhaustion and had gone bankrupt because of Letterman's actions.

The New Mexico statute appears to limit domestic violence to "any incident by a household member," and Letterman, who lives in Connecticut and works in New York, had never been in Nestler's household. But New Mexico law defines household member to include "a person with whom the petitioner has had a continuing personal relationship," and Nestler's charge that Letterman's broadcast of television messages for 11 years qualified as a "continuing" relationship and thereby turned him into a household member.

The family court judge who issued the order, Daniel Sanchez, might have been predisposed to believe any allegation presented to him by a complaining woman even though she had no evidence. His own biography lists him as chairman of the Northern New Mexico Domestic Violence Task Force.

Violence Should Require Overt Acts

RADAR reports that only five states define domestic violence in terms of overt actions that can be objectively proven or refuted in a court of law. The rest of the states have broadened their definition to include fear, emotional distress, and psychological feelings.

The use of the word "harassment" in domestic violence definitions is borrowed from the Equal Employment Opportunity Commission's definition, which is based on the "effect" of an action rather than the action itself. In Oklahoma, a man can be charged with harassment if he seriously "annoys" a woman.

Feminists Expand "Domestic Violence"

The 1999 book by University of Massachusetts Professor Daphne Patai, *Heterophobia: Sexual Harassment and the Future of Feminism*, powerfully indicts what she labels the "Sexual Harassment Industry." Feminists have created a judicial world in which accusation equals guilt, and the distinction between severe offenses and trivial annoyances is erased.

RADAR's report explains that the definition of *domestic* has also been expanded. Originally, domestic meant a house-

False Allegations Help Win Custody

The domestic violence industry was hijacked by the feminists around 30 years ago; however, perhaps the most damaging process took place some 15 years ago, namely the "fusing" of the domestic violence industry with the divorce industry. Simply stated, women know, and are often advised by their attorneys, that if they want to get custody of the children, they had better try to nail dad with some sort of domestic violence accusation. In many states, that alone will nail the coffin.

The National Father's Resource Center, 2008.

hold member, but now it means a person with whom the woman "has been involved in an intimate relationship" (Colorado), people who are in a "dating or engagement relationship" (Rhode Island), or "any other person . . . as determined by the court" (North Dakota).

How did it happen that state laws against domestic violence are written so broadly as to produce such absurdities? Family court judges issue 2 million temporary restraining orders every year, half of which are routinely extended, 85 percent are against men, and half do not include any allegation of violence but rely on vague complaints made without evidence.

Follow the money, both at the supply and the demand ends of the economic trail. The supply of 1,500 new domestic violence laws enacted by states from 1997 to 2005 is largely the handiwork of targeted lobbying by feminists funded by the multimillion-dollar federal boondoggle called the Violence Against Women Act.

Financial Incentives to Lie or Exaggerate

The act is blatantly gender discriminatory; as its title proclaims, it is designed to address only complaints by women. The Violence Against Women Act provides taxpayer funding to feminists to teach legislators, judges and prosecutors the stereotypes that men are batterers and women are victims.

The demand end of the economic chain is the fact that women know (and their lawyers advise them) that making allegations of domestic violence (even without proof or evidence) is the fastest and cheapest way to win child custody plus generous financial support. The financial incentives to lie or exaggerate are powerful.

Due Process Violated

Due process violations in the issuing of temporary restraining orders include lack of notice, no presumption of innocence, denial of poor defendants to free counsel while women are given taxpayer-funded support, denial of the right to take depositions, lack of evidentiary hearings, improper standard of proof, no need to be found guilty beyond a reasonable doubt, denial of the right to confront accusers, and denial of trial by jury.

Assault and battery are already crimes in every state without any need of the Violence Against Women Act. Temporary restraining orders empower activist family court judges to criminalize a vast range of otherwise legal behavior (usually a father's contact with his own children and entry into his own home), which are crimes only for the recipient of the order, who can then be arrested and jailed without trial for doing what no statute prohibits and what anyone else may lawfully do.

"Serious violence between siblings is disturbingly common and much more prevalent than serious child abuse by parents."

Sibling Abuse Is a Serious Domestic Violence Problem

Mark S. Kiselica and Mandy Morrill-Richards

In the following viewpoint, Mark S. Kiselica and Mandy Morrill-Richards argue that sibling abuse affects more people than any other type of domestic violence. Parents, the authors say, often cannot distinguish between sibling rivalry and sibling abuse. Sibling abuse can be psychological, physical, or sexual and is strongly associated with violence in future relationships, according to Kiselica and Morrill-Richards. The authors also claim that sibling incest may be the most common form of sexual abuse perpetrated by family members. Mark S. Kiselica is a faculty member at the College of New Jersey, and Mandy Morrill-Richards is a faculty member at the University of Memphis.

Mark S. Kiselica and Mandy Morrill-Richards, "Sibling Maltreatment: The Forgotten Abuse," *Journal of Counseling and Development*, March 22, 2007. Copyright © 2007 American Counseling Association. Reprinted with permission. No further reproduction authorized without written permission from the American Counseling Association.

As you read, consider the following questions:

1. According to figures quoted by the authors, what percentage of children aged three to seventeen have committed acts of severe violence against a sibling?

2. According to Kiselica and Morrill-Richards, how does emotional sibling abuse affect self-esteem of victims and perpetrators?

3. According to figures cited by the authors, what percentage of women have been sexually victimized by a sibling?

Data reported in several studies over the past 3 decades suggest that sibling abuse is pandemic and can have fatal results. For example, [M.A.] Straus, [R.J.] Gelles, and [S.K.] Steinmetz found that as many as 40% of children in the United States engage in physical aggression against siblings, and as many as 85% engage in verbal aggression against siblings on a regular basis. [V.R.] Wiehe estimated that as many as 53 out of every 100 children are perpetrators of sibling abuse. [M.P.] Goodwin and [B.] Roscoe used the Conflict Tactics Incidence Scale to measure the frequency of abuse in families among 272 high school students, and they found that 60% of the participants reported being either a victim or a perpetrator of sibling abuse. In their national surveys of 8,145 families, Straus and Gelles reported that 80% of children ages 3 to 17 years commit some form of violence against a sibling. The most recent data [from the Federal Bureau of Investigation] regarding homicide in the United States indicate that siblings perpetrated 6.1% of all murders committed by family members in 2002. These statistics are startling and point out that sibling relationships can be marred by violence.

The pervasive nature of sibling abuse can be better understood when it is considered in relation to data regarding officially verified cases of severe intrafamily abuse. Approximately 1% of children in the United States are severely abused by a parent, 1.8% of adult women experience extreme abuse by an intimate partner, and 3% to 5% of older adults experience some form of family-based elder abuse. Unfortunately, [according to Wiehe,] national statistics based on reported cases of sibling abuse "do not exist because generally cases of physical or emotional sibling abuse do not come to the attention of authorities." However, extensive national survey data reveal that serious violence between siblings is disturbingly common and much more prevalent than serious child abuse by parents: 53% of children ages 3 to 17 years have committed acts of severe violence (such as punching, kicking, stabbing, or attacking with objects) against a brother or sister, whereas only 2.3% of parents have engaged in severe violence toward their children. Collectively, these data suggest that sibling maltreatment might be the most common form of intrafamily abuse. Indeed, Straus and Gelles, the authors of the most definitive study of violence in families in the United States ever undertaken, concluded, "Children are the most violent persons in American families."

Sibling relationships are ubiquitous. [J.] Caffaro and [A.] Conn-Caffaro found that 83% of the adult population in the United States was raised with at least one sibling in the family. Adults typically have more siblings than children, and, compared with statistics in the past, a greater percentage of current adults do not marry or marry at a later age. These findings indicate that the sibling relationship is unique in its longevity and can be one of the most influential relationships in one's life. Therefore, the impact siblings have on one another should not be minimized.

Causes of Sibling Abuse

Why does sibling abuse occur? Authorities on the subject have proposed that maladaptive parental behavior and dysfunctional family structures play key roles in the genesis of sibling abuse. Parental treatment has an impact on the sibling relationship. When the family structure supports power imbalances, rigid gender roles, differential treatment of siblings, and lack of parental supervision, there is an increased risk for sibling abuse. In a study conducted by Wiehe, the normalization of abuse by parents was found to be a key factor in the severity and frequency of abuse between siblings. When parents are unable to make the distinction between normal sibling rivalry and sibling abuse, it can lead to other risk factors, such as the inappropriate expression of anger from one sibling toward another. Parents may encourage this behavior as a form of release or ventilation of anger, which usually has the effect of promoting aggression rather than easing hostility in the child. Several studies have found a link between child abuse and the delinquent behavior of siblings. It has been shown that an abused child may inflict abuse on a sibling because he or she is modeling the actions of his or her parents.

The tolerance of sibling abuse can have devastating results for both the victim and the perpetrator. . . .

Psychological Abuse

Psychological abuse can have serious long-term consequences if parents minimize the importance of abusive actions between siblings and do not seek help for their children. It is important for counselors to take reports of psychological abuse seriously and to observe the behavior of siblings. If the abuse is not addressed, victims may internalize abusive messages. Children who experience psychological abuse may act out by crying or screaming or hide in an attempt to isolate themselves from the abuser. It has been shown that there is a connection between experiencing emotional abuse as a child and developing habit disorders, conduct disorders, neurotic traits, and psychoneurotic reactions; experiencing lags in development; and attempting to commit suicide. In addition, both the victims and the perpetrators of emotional sibling abuse tend to have significantly lower levels of self-esteem as

Sibling Abuse More Common

Not a lot of parents or teachers know to look for it, but sibling abuse affects 50 percent of all children. With sibling homicides making up one percent of all cases in the last decade according to the FBI, sibling abuse is probably more common than child abuse by a parent or spousal abuse. Most of us look at adults as the dangerous or aggressive members of American families, but children are actually the most violent.

Dentalplans.com, May 23, 2006.
www.dentalplans.com/articles/Sibling_Abuse_or_Rivalry.

adults than do nonvictims. Psychological abuse is also present in both physical and sexual sibling abuse.

Sibling Violence Is Most Common

Physical abuse by a sibling is defined as one member of the sibling pair deliberately causing physical harm to the other member. The harm may be inflicted by shoving, hitting, slapping, kicking, biting, pinching, scratching, and hair pulling. More severe forms of physical abuse by siblings include the use of broom handles, rubber hoses, coat hangers, hairbrushes, belts, sticks, knives, guns and rifles, broken glass, razor blades, and scissors to inflict injury and pain. Some victims have reported that their siblings attempted to drown them, nearly suffocated them with a pillow, or repeatedly hit them in the stomach until they lost their breath.

Sibling violence is the most common form of intimate violence in the United States. [C.] Simonelli, [V.] Mullis, [A.] Elliott, and [T.] Pierce found that approximately two thirds of 120 college students experienced physical violence from a sibling, and 3.4% reported being threatened by a sibling with a gun or a knife. The results of a national survey of family violence indicated that 80% of children between the ages of 3 and 17 had hit a brother or a sister, and more than half have engaged in severe acts of violence, such as punching, kicking, stabbing, or hitting with an object.

Age is an important factor to consider in relation to sibling violence because the severity of and the motivation for the abuse change over time. Children under the age of 8 years tend to use physical violence to resolve conflicts over possessions. Adolescents between the ages of 9 and 13 years use physical violence to declare spatial boundaries. Teenagers over the age of 14 years use physical violence to deal with conflict over responsibilities and social obligations. Physical violence between siblings usually declines with age, which may lead parents to dismiss the acts and minimize the impact of the aggressive interactions on the siblings. There is a high probability that the abused child will experience additional abuse later in life if there is no intervention. In particular, there is a strong association between sibling abuse and subsequent experiences of violence within dating relationships.

Sibling Incest Is Most Common

Sibling incest might be the most common form of sexual abuse perpetrated by immediate family members. The U.S. Department of Health and Human Services reported [in 2002] that approximately 0.12% of children are sexually abused by an adult family member; by comparison, at least 23,000 out of every 1,000,000 women (2.3%) have been sexually victimized by a sibling.

Sibling incest is defined as sexual behavior between siblings that is not age appropriate, not transitory, and not motivated by developmentally appropriate curiosity. Sexual abuse between siblings is not limited to intercourse. It has been shown that unwanted sexual advances, sexual leers, and forcing a sibling to view pornographic material can have as much of a psychological impact on the victim as actual intercourse.

Impact of Sibling Incest Underestimated

The impact and prevalence of sibling incest is often underestimated by society. This may be because of the difficulty in establishing the victim and offender roles. Determining if coercion was a factor in the abuse may be another obstacle when dealing with siblings. Another difference between adult and sibling abuse is that no generational boundary has been violated, and this makes sexual abuse easier to hide. An exaggerated sexual climate in the family or a rigidly repressive sexual family environment increases the risk of sibling sexual abuse. These environments may also involve multiple perpetrators of sexual abuse within the family, which makes detecting and dealing with the sexual abuse of a sibling even more difficult. Each offender may use denial as a means to protect him- or herself from experiencing shame and to maintain the abuse, so the likelihood of any one member of the family reporting the incest is reduced.

Children who experience sibling incest exhibit a wide variety of psychological problems. Sexual sibling abuse creates fear, anger, shame, humiliation, and guilt. Many children who have been sexually abused by a sibling learn to connect victimization with sex and have difficulty separating pleasure from pain and fear from desire in a sexual relationship when they become adults.

Counseling for the Whole Family

How the family reacts when the existence of sibling sexual abuse is disclosed plays an important part in the recovery of the victim. Often it is difficult for families to seek appropriate help because of shame, fear, and disbelief that sexual abuse is occurring. Some families may attempt to address sibling sexual abuse without seeking the assistance of resources outside of the family. Without counseling, education, and support for all members of the family, it is unlikely that sibling sexual abuse will end.

> "[There are] higher rates of domestic
> violence involving same-sex couples
> than heterosexual ones."

Same-Sex Domestic Violence Is a Serious Problem

Tod W. Burke and Stephen S. Owen

In the following viewpoint, Tod W. Burke and Stephen S. Owen argue that same-sex domestic violence is a greater problem than heterosexual domestic violence. Same-sex domestic violence also has unique features, say the authors, such as threatening to "out" the victim. Unlike heterosexual domestic violence, size and strength inequalities often are not indicators of the danger of same-sex domestic violence or identifiers of the likely abuser. Domestic violence laws, the authors contend, need to apply to same-sex couples, and police need training in same-sex domestic violence. Tod W. Burke is a professor of criminal justice and Stephen S. Owen is an assistant professor of criminal justice at Radford University.

As you read, consider the following questions:

1. According to figures quoted by the authors, what percentages of gay men and lesbians have experienced domestic violence?

2. According to Burke and Owen, whom do abusers tend to blame for their own violent behavior?

3. In the authors' view, how does the tendency to treat gays and lesbians as a marginalized population affect the problem of same-sex domestic violence?

Domestic violence is understood to be the use of any instrumentality to control a household member, including physical harm or its threat, isolation from friends and family, economic deprivation, sexual assaults, destruction of property, withholding medication, and psychological manipulation. While few studies that have been conducted on same-sex domestic violence support the conclusion, it is widespread among both gay and lesbian couples. One early study reported that some 47 percent of gays and lesbians have been victimized by domestic violence. Others have suggested that from 42 to 79 percent of men and 25 to fifty percent of women in same-sex relationships have experienced some form of domestic violence. These statistics support a 2003 analysis of the National Criminal Victimization Survey, which pointed to higher rates of domestic violence involving same-sex couples than heterosexual ones.

Threat of "Outing" as a Weapon

Underlying this difference is the fact that domestic violence itself varies somewhat between same-sex and heterosexual couples. For example, "outing" one's partner is not an issue for heterosexuals but is a surprisingly common weapon for gay people in an abusive relationship. This may appear trivial to some, but many gay men and lesbians wish to keep their sexual orientation private for fear of retaliation, such as loss of one's job or estrangement from family and friends. Same-sex domestic violence can also be complicated by the issue of HIV. We certainly recognize that HIV is not confined to the gay community, but there have been a number of reports of individuals deliberately infecting a partner in an effort to prevent the victim from leaving the relationship. Some abusers may even withhold medication or prevent their sick partner from seeking treatment. Others have been known to threaten to notify the victim's employer, parents, and friends of his HIV status.

Abuser or Victim?

Another difference is that it's often harder to distinguish the abuser from the victim in same-sex domestic violence. Being a batterer or victim is not determined by a person's size or strength. This is particularly important to understand when law enforcement personnel confront same-sex domestic violence situations. For instance, police officers may assume that since two males are involved, both are of equal strength and can therefore handle the problem without their intervention. This assumption is not only wrong, but it could be deadly, both for the victim and the officers. This ambiguity can be partially overcome if we understand the typical profile of both the batterer and the victim. Profiling is a process whereby people are placed into categories based upon shared characteristics. This method is somewhat controversial, and there's no doubt that caution should be exercised when one attempts to comprehend a given relationship based on certain personality traits that have been identified. We can, however, make some generalizations based upon past behavior and research.

Both batterers and victims come from all socioeconomic, ethnic, educational, occupational, and religious backgrounds, as well as all age groups. The typical characteristics of abusers include self-hatred, depression, insecurity, poor communication skills, low self-control, jealousy, and manipulativeness.

Not Just a Heterosexual Problem

- Between ¼ and ⅓ of all LGBT [lesbian, gay, bisexual, and transgender] individuals experience domestic violence.

- Partner abuse occurs within the LGBT community with the same frequency and severity as it does among heterosexuals. It may begin as emotional and verbal abuse and commonly escalates into physical violence that can be life threatening.

Pacific Pride Foundation, 2007. www.pacificpridefoundation.org.

Many batterers have a history of battering and violence, as well as alcohol and/or drug abuse. Needless to say, alcohol is known to trigger or escalate violent situations. One trait many abusers have in common is a tendency to blame the victim for their own violent behavior.

Victims tend to share certain characteristics, as well. These may include self-blame, conflict avoidance, low trust in others, low self-esteem, depression, fear of abandonment, among others. Many victims are people who feel uncomfortable with disagreement; many tend to deny or minimize the abuse; a large proportion feel "trapped" in the relationship for financial or emotional reasons. Victims often develop ways to mollify or avoid the abuser. They often find that leaving the abuser is difficult. If they do leave, they often return, feeling guilty about having left the relationship, or because they believe they can "save" the abuser.

Cycle of Violence

When does the violence stop? This is a difficult question, but we have come to believe that in general the violence doesn't stop until the victim leaves the relationship for good. Abuse is rarely a one-time occurrence, and it is unlikely to change once a pattern has been established—not impossible with a proper treatment program, but few couples will ever seek help.

Many victims experience a "cycle of violence" that typically involves three stages of abuse. The first is a tension-building stage that may result in constant arguing or "the silent treatment." If violence does occur, it is usually restricted to what the law refers to as "simple assault," causing only minor injuries. This stage may last from days to years. The next phase is known as the "acute battering" stage. The violence increases in severity and the victim may be punched, kicked, slapped, choked, etc., resulting in observable bruises, lesions, or broken bones. This stage may last anywhere from a few minutes to days. The final stage in the cycle is a "calming" stage in which the abuser is apologetic, begging forgiveness and promising never to repeat the violence. The abuser often showers the victim with presents in an attempt to gain forgiveness. With each new cycle in a relationship, the severity of the violence is likely to increase, while the duration of the cycle will decrease.

Stopping the Violence

What can be done to stop the abuse? From a social policy standpoint, a number of steps are needed. First, domestic violence laws must include same-sex couples. Second, criminal justice personnel need adequate training and education. The police need to be more sensitive to the needs of the gay and lesbian community, particularly when enforcing domestic violence laws. While some police agencies have incorporated diversity training into their training programs, many officers fail to take these programs seriously. Officers need to be able to provide information concerning available resources, assist victims in developing a safety plan, and aid victims in obtaining restraining orders against the abuser. Some police agencies in large cities have appointed community liaison officers who meet with representatives within the gay and lesbian community to address their concerns.

Prosecutors must pursue cases of same-sex domestic violence. Judges also need to become more sensitive and aware of same-sex domestic violence. For instance, one judge modified an abused gay man's restraining order from one year to three months when the judge discovered that the victim of the abuse had a black belt in karate. The judge commented that the victim could "take care of himself." Judges must also avoid sentence disparity based upon sexual orientation.

Safe Houses and Counseling

Resources and funding need to be made available, including short- and long-term support. Safe houses and shelters, places where a victim can stay to escape his abuser, must be provided. Currently safe houses are rarely accessible to same-sex domestic victims, particularly males. Some locales provide safe houses that exclude pets. Victims of domestic violence sometimes refuse to leave the relationship for fear that their pet may be harmed (abusers may harm or threaten harm to a pet as a means to control the victim). Indeed research has also shown a strong relationship between domestic violence and pet abuse!

Counseling needs to be available for both victims and abusers in same-sex domestic violence relationships. We strongly recommend individual or group counseling rather than couples counseling, which has proven to be not only ineffective but potentially dangerous to the victim once the session is complete. The abuser must receive treatment and counseling to recognize the source of his or her violent behavior, and learn to deal with conflict in a nonviolent manner. Otherwise, the pattern is likely to continue. And the gay and lesbian community must discuss same-sex domestic violence openly. This can be accomplished through supportive politicians, gay and lesbian media outlets, notices in gay and lesbian bars and clubs, discussion seminars, and community meetings, to name a few.

The problem is exacerbated by the current political climate, which treats gays and lesbians as a marginalized population. It is our hope that this piece will spark concern and promote action by gay and lesbian organizations and individuals to address this under-reported but widespread social ill that afflicts our community.

> *"As many as 275 million children world-wide are exposed to violence in the home."*

Domestic Violence Harms Children

UNICEF

In the following viewpoint, UNICEF contends that children who witness domestic violence in the home are seriously harmed. Negative effects can include increased likelihood of child abuse, behavioral problems, and delinquency, the organization claims. In addition, children exposed to domestic violence are likely to perpetrate or be victims of domestic violence when they become adults. UNICEF, the United Nations Children's Fund, works to help children overcome the obstacles of poverty, violence, disease, and discrimination in countries throughout the world.

As you read, consider the following questions:

1. According to UNICEF, why is it difficult to collect reliable data on children exposed to domestic violence?

2. According to figures cited by the author, what percentage of children victimized by child abuse also report violence in the home?

UNICEF, "Behind Closed Doors: The Impact of Domestic Violence on Children," 2006. Reproduced by permission.

3. What is the single best predictor of children becoming either perpetrators or victims of domestic violence later in life, according to UNICEF?

What do children need? We know the answer from our own childhoods. First and foremost, children need a safe and secure home, free of violence, and parents that love and protect them. They need to have a sense of routine and stability, so that when things go wrong in the outside world, home is a place of comfort, help and support.

For too many children, home is far from a safe haven. Every year, hundreds of millions of children are exposed to domestic violence at home, and this has a powerful and profound impact on their lives and hopes for the future. These children not only watch one parent violently assaulting another, they often hear the distressing sounds of violence, or may be aware of it from many telltale signs.

"Me and my sister are scared," says one nine-year-old girl who lives in a violent home in the United Kingdom. "Our parents fight a lot and we fear they might split up. They fight when we're upstairs. They don't think we know what's going on, but we do."

Impact on Children

Violence in the home is one of the most pervasive human rights challenges of our time. It remains a largely hidden problem that few countries, communities or families openly confront. Violence in the home is not limited by geography, ethnicity, or status; it is a global phenomenon.

The devastating effects of domestic violence on women are well documented. Far less is known about the impact on children who witness a parent or caregiver being subjected to violence. These children—the forgotten victims of violence in the home—are the focus of this report.

The findings show that children who are exposed to violence in the home may suffer a range of severe and lasting effects. Children who grow up in a violent home are more likely to be victims of child abuse. Those who are not direct victims have some of the same behavioural and psychological problems as children who are themselves physically abused.

Children who are exposed to violence in the home may have difficulty learning and limited social skills, exhibit violent, risky or delinquent behaviour, or suffer from depression or severe anxiety. Children in the earliest years of life are particularly vulnerable: studies show that domestic violence is more prevalent in homes with younger children than those with older children.

Several studies also reveal that children who witness domestic violence are more likely to be affected by violence as adults—either as victims or perpetrators.

Children who are exposed to violence in the home are denied their right to a safe and stable home environment. Many are suffering silently, and with little support. Children who are exposed to violence in the home need trusted adults to turn to for help and comfort, and services that will help them to cope with their experiences. Far more must be done to protect these children and to prevent domestic violence from happening in the first place. . . .

Extent of Problem

Collecting reliable data on this hidden issue poses several challenges. In almost every country there is limited data available on the prevalence of domestic violence, and even less information on the numbers of children who may be exposed to such violence. Some countries have no data at all. The studies themselves often acknowledge that their findings are limited by underreporting of domestic violence, both by the abused parent and by children who live in the home.

Despite these limitations, the research provides what we believe is a first, critical step toward a fuller picture of how many children are exposed to violence in the home.

Worldwide Domestic Violence Victims

Between 133 and 275 million children worldwide are estimated to witness domestic violence annually. The exposure of children to violence in their homes on a frequent basis, usually through fights between parents or between a mother and her partner, can severely affect a child's well-being, personal development and social interaction in childhood and adulthood. Intimate partner violence also increases the risk of violence against children in the family, with studies from China, Colombia, Egypt, Mexico, the Philippines and South Africa showing a strong relationship between violence against women with violence against children. A study from India found that domestic violence in the home doubled the risk of violence against children.

United Nations Secretary-General's Study,
"Violence Against Children," 2006.
www.unviolencestudy.org.

The numbers estimated by the research are staggering. As many as 275 million children worldwide are exposed to violence in the home. This range is a conservative estimate based on the limitations of the available data. In actuality, millions more children may be affected by violence in the home. . . .

Risk of Child Abuse

There is a common link between domestic violence and child abuse. Among victims of child abuse, 40 per cent report domestic violence in the home. One study in North America found that children who were exposed to violence in the home were 15 times more likely to be physically and/or sexually assaulted than the national average. This link has been confirmed around the world, with supporting studies from a range of countries including China, South Africa, Colombia, India, Egypt, the Philippines, and Mexico.

Risk to Development

Infants and small children who are exposed to violence in the home experience so much added emotional stress that it can harm the development of their brains and impair cognitive and sensory growth. Behaviour changes can include excessive irritability, sleep problems, emotional distress, fear of being alone, immature behaviour, and problems with toilet training and language development. At an early age, a child's brain is becoming 'hard-wired' for later physical and emotional functioning. Exposure to domestic violence threatens that development.

As they grow, children who are exposed to violence may continue to show signs of problems. Primary-school-age children may have more trouble with school work, and show poor concentration and focus. They tend not to do as well in school. In one study, forty per cent had lower reading abilities than children from non-violent homes.

Personality and behavioural problems among children exposed to violence in the home can take the forms of psychosomatic illnesses, depression, suicidal tendencies, and bedwetting. Later in life, these children are at greater risk for substance abuse, juvenile pregnancy and criminal behaviour than those raised in homes without violence.

Some studies suggest social development is also damaged. Some children lose the ability to feel empathy for others. Others feel socially isolated, unable to make friends as easily due to social discomfort or confusion over what is acceptable. Many studies have noted that children from violent homes exhibit signs of more aggressive behaviour, such as bullying, and are up to three times more likely to be involved in fighting.

One Australian study showed that up to 40 per cent of chronically violent teenagers have been exposed to extreme domestic violence.

Continuing Cycle of Violence

The single best predictor of children becoming either perpetrators or victims of domestic violence later in life is whether or not they grow up in a home where there is domestic violence. Studies from various countries support the findings that rates of abuse are higher among women whose husbands were abused as children or who saw their mothers being abused. Children who grow up with violence in the home learn early and powerful lessons about the use of violence in interpersonal relationships to dominate others, and might even be encouraged in doing so.

| *"Young adults often don't realize that jealousy and control aren't signs of love but abuse."*

Domestic Violence Is a Problem for College Students

Peggy O'Hare

In the following viewpoint, Peggy O'Hare argues that college students are especially vulnerable to domestic violence. Young adults, away from their support network at home for the first time, don't know how to identify or deal with unhealthy relationships, she states. College students often rationalize or downplay controlling behaviors that are warning signs of potential domestic violence. Fear and shame, according to O'Hare, also discourage victims from reporting harassment. Peggy O'Hare writes for the Houston Chronicle.

As you read, consider the following questions:

1. In the two slayings described by the author at the beginning of the article, what behaviors did both of the perpetrators exhibit towards the victims during the months preceding the murders?

2. What age group, according to a study cited by O'Hare, has the highest average annual rate for intimate partner victimization not resulting in death?

3. According to the University of Texas counselor quoted by the author, what is the best thing college students can do to stay safe?

Enrolled at different universities, Tynesha Stewart and Rachel Pendray both aimed for lofty futures—Stewart in the engineering field, Pendray in nursing. Both balanced extracurricular activities with their studies and had wide circles of friends.

And, according to those closest to them, both suffered persistent harassment from men whose lives were going nowhere—Stewart from an unemployed ex-boyfriend eight years her senior, Pendray from a former fellow student whose romantic affections she did not reciprocate.

Both women thought they could handle the excessive, unwanted attention and never reported the harassment to police or university officials. But both lives ended tragically and violently.

Pendray, a 20-year-old Sam Houston State University cheerleader, died when a man whose romantic advances she rejected shot her seven times, then turned the gun on himself at her Huntsville apartment.

Investigators found a possible bite mark shaped like a horseshoe on Pendray's thigh and bruises to her lower extremities but no evidence that she had been sexually assaulted or was sexually active, an autopsy showed.

Stewart, 19, a Texas A&M University freshman, vanished during spring break after leaving her mother's home with an ex-boyfriend who later confessed to choking her. Authorities say the killer dismembered Stewart's remains and burned them on barbecue pits at his north Harris County apartment.

College Students Are Vulnerable

The two cases, though vastly different in many respects, highlight the complex problems of domestic violence, stalking and harassment, as well as the unhealthy interactions or relationships that precede such crimes.

Both suspects demonstrated patterns of trying to control their victims in the months before the slayings, such as checking their whereabouts, calling incessantly, sending numerous text messages or displaying inappropriate fits of anger, friends say.

College students are particularly vulnerable to such volatile relationships, experts say, because they are away from their support network at home, aren't aware of how to identify or deal with unhealthy interactions and tend to downplay the warning signs.

Students that age also typically think they are invulnerable or immune to crime, other observers say.

"I firmly believe there's a lack of awareness of what is healthy or unhealthy in dating relationships," said Ashley Teitelbaum, public outreach chair for the Brazos County Coalition Against Domestic Violence, an advocacy group in the same county as Texas A&M.

Women 20–24 posted the highest average annual rate among all age groups for intimate partner victimization not resulting in death, according to a study released in December by the U.S. Bureau of Justice Statistics.

That trend is no different in Texas, where this age group ranked highest in 2005 in the number of family-violence victims and offenders, a Texas Department of Public Safety report found.

Even more alarming, this activity appears to be increasing.

Recent studies suggest up to one in three college couples will experience at least one violent incident during their dating relationships, according to a 2006 article in the *Journal of Interpersonal Violence*, "Dating Violence Among College Men and Women."

And a college-oriented survey taken in 2004 indicates 2.4 percent of college women and 1.3 percent of men reported being in relationships marked by physical abuse.

Controlling Behavior

Stewart's history with Timothy Wayne Shepherd, 27, who confessed to killing her in March, was plagued by troubling signs during their two-year courtship.

The slain woman's sister recalled an occasion when Shepherd shook Stewart by the shoulders and another when Stewart had a bruise on her arm. Stewart downplayed that, saying Shepherd had just "pushed" her.

Her family also said Shepherd once flooded and spray-painted the inside of an apartment rented in Stewart's name when he became angry she wasn't spending enough time with him. Shepherd called her up to 10 times a day before her fatal trip home for spring break, her roommate told the *Houston Chronicle*.

Pendray had far less history with her killer, Jacob Robert Taylor, 24, of Houston.

The pair had gone on only a couple of dates, her best friend said, but Pendray spurned Taylor's wishes to become romantic.

Taylor also never became violent toward Pendray prior to killing her and himself in December. Yet the harassment Pendray suffered at his hands was no less intense.

Taylor "felt like she was obligated to call him," said Pendray's best friend, Sarah Sheffield, of Houston. "On at least 10 occasions, he would call me asking weird questions— 'Where is she? Why doesn't she return my phone calls? Why doesn't she like me?'

Teens Need Help for Dating Abuse

Domestic abuse workers have long known younger women are victims of [dating] abuse. From 2001 to 2005, women ages 20 to 24 reported the highest rates of domestic and dating non-fatal violence, according to the Bureau of Justice Statistics. Teen girls had rates similar to women ages 25 to 34. . . .

At the [National Teen Dating Abuse] helpline, callers often seek advice not on filing a protective order, but on telling their parents about being hit or arranging safe places at school away from an abusive classmate they had been dating. Others call with questions about Web stalking or being harassed through text messaging.

Sarah Viren, "Abuse Helpline Goes Tech-Savvy for Teens—Texas Takes a Youthful Approach to Effort to End Dating Violence," February 8, 2008. www.ncdsv.org.

"I just thought it was sort of strange that he always wanted to know where she was."

Advocates say such controlling behaviors can be "red flags" of more serious problems to come.

Yet, they say, college students tend to rationalize such warning signs or dismiss them as personality quirks.

"It's something we really try to impress upon students—to pay attention to these flags and not deny them, not minimize them," said Heather Davies, a counseling specialist with the University of Texas' Voices Against Violence program, which helps students victimized by relationship violence, sexual assaults or stalking.

Women often have trouble ceasing contact with suitors who display controlling or jealous behavior, but cutting off communication is wise if a situation escalates, Davies said.

"Women in particular are socialized in our society to be pleasant and to be nice, and if we say no, to say no in ways that other people just kind of run right over it," Davies said. "So the concept or idea of saying, 'Oh, I don't have to call him back or take his call?' is just revolutionary to students."

Young adults often don't realize that jealousy and control aren't signs of love but abuse, advocates say. Complicating the situation, young adults' relationships aren't taken as seriously.

"We don't hold them to the same standards as adult relationships. We tend to look at them as trials," said Kelly Boros, communications manager for the Houston Area Women's Center.

Fear and Shame Fuel Silence

There's no way to accurately track the frequency of domestic violence and harassment among the college-student population because that demographic tends to shy away from reporting such incidents to authorities, observers say.

This reluctance is true not only for victims but for fellow students who witness the problems, said a former director of Texas A&M's Women's and Gender Equity Center.

"At A&M . . . there was a lot of reluctance to report because (students) wouldn't want to ruin someone's life," said Brenda Bethman, who left the school in January to become director of the University of Missouri-Kansas City Women's Center.

Victims also remain silent out of fear and shame, advocates say. Others who see their suffering may not report the harassment because they consider it "private," Bethman said.

At the University of Texas [UT], however, the number of reported incidents has increased since the school launched the Voices Against Violence program at its Counseling and Mental Health Center in 2002, said program director Jane Morgan Bost.

In the first four years of operation, UT students reported 567 sexual assaults, 381 incidents of domestic violence and 96 incidents of stalking, Morgan Bost said. Last year [2006] alone, UT students reported 122 sexual assaults, 91 incidents of relationship violence and 22 stalking incidents, she said.

All of the victims were students, most were women, and the majority of the incidents reported occurred off campus, Morgan Bost said.

The numbers were captured from multiple sources and are not considered a complete account since some incidents likely were never reported, she said.

UT's numbers have risen not because of increased crime, Morgan Bost says, but because heightened awareness has led more students to speak up.

Online Stalking

Despite the sense of security that pervades college campuses, technology has allowed perpetrators to up the ante on their victims in such settings.

"With the use of the Internet, we're just seeing huge increases in cyberstalking," said Davies, the counseling specialist at UT. ". . . We've definitely noticed (harassment on) things like Facebook and My Space and cell phones and text messages."

There are vast resources available to college students caught up in such situations.

If victims don't want to contact police, they can seek counseling on campus, contact local women's centers or alert university officials who can take administrative action, especially if the perpetrator is a fellow student.

Counselors also can help victims form a safety plan and advise them how to protect themselves without further aggravating an unstable situation.

But no matter the surroundings or the circumstances, the best thing students can do is heed their instincts, Davies said.

"If your gut tells you to feel afraid," she said, "listen to it."

"Stress, frustration, and feelings of burden experienced by caregivers who are caring for dependent elders can result in abusive and neglectful treatment."

Domestic Violence Is a Problem for the Elderly

Denise A. Hines and Kathleen Malley-Morrison

In the following viewpoint, Denise A. Hines and Kathleen Malley-Morrison argue that domestic violence against the elderly is a serious problem. Many abusers, the authors contend, are dependent upon the victim financially and may have emotional or substance abuse problems. Frail elderly females are especially vulnerable to elder abuse, they assert. Often elders are unwilling to take steps to end the violence due to dependence upon or love for the abuser. Denise A. Hines is a research fellow at the University of New Hampshire and Kathleen Malley-Morrison is a professor of psychology at Boston University specializing in family violence.

As you read, consider the following questions:

1. In what percentage of cases in which elderly wives are physically abused do injuries occur, according to figures quoted by the authors?

2. According to a Wisconsin study cited by Hines and Malley-Morrison, what percentage of abusers were living in the elder's home at the time of the abuse?

3. Which gender is more likely to perpetrate abuse of elders, according to data cited by the authors?

According to the NEAIS [National Elder Abuse Incidence Study] data, [elder] abuse by spouses is more likely to go unreported than reported; only 19% of cases reported to APS [Adult Protective Services] compared to 30.3% of unreported cases are committed by spouses. In the random sample survey of elder abuse in Boston, *nearly three fifths* of the perpetrators were spouses. Yet even though a substantial percentage of elder abusers are spouses, this type of abuse has been the least researched. Perhaps, as [K.] Pillemer and [D.] Finkelhor suggested, the reason for this lack of attention is because elderly spouses hitting each other does not conjure up the same abhorrent images as does the situation of a stronger, healthier, middle-aged adult hitting an elder. Moreover, although many people probably assume that the consequences of spousal elder abuse are not as severe as other forms of elder abuse, Pillemer and Finkelhor's data show otherwise: According to their study, there were no differences in the level of violence committed, the number of injuries sustained, or the degree of upset engendered in the victim between cases where the abuser was a spouse versus those where the abuser was an adult child. Because the elderly are much more likely to live with their spouses only than with their adult children only, this area of spousal elder abuse needs more attention.

Rate of Elder Abuse by Spouses

The rate of abuse by elderly spouses may be as much as 41 per 1,000 elders. Other studies have shown that between 4% and 6% of elders are involved in physically abusive spousal relationships. Injuries have been shown to occur in as many as 6% of physically abused elderly husbands and 57% of physically abused elderly wives. However, even though these rates are quite substantial, little effort has been made to protect these elderly victims of spousal abuse, probably because neither the spousal abuse nor the elder abuse system is specifically designed to deal with this form of maltreatment. Spousal abuse programs are designed with young couples in mind, and elder abuse programs are designed around the notion that caretaking relatives are abusing the elders. Therefore, even though the elderly victims of spousal abuse should conceivably have two systems to turn to for help or to investigate their plights, they often fall through the cracks.

Stressed Caregivers

In contrast to spousal elder abuse, the abuse of elders by adult relatives who are entrusted with their care is the most researched and most widely recognized type of elder abuse. Statistics compiled by APS, as seen in the NEAIS, indicate that frail, confused, elderly women over the age of 80 are the most likely group to experience elder abuse, primarily at the hands of family members. According to work by [S.K.] Steinmetz, these elderly reside in the homes of their middle-aged children, who must adjust their lifestyles to accommodate to this new responsibility. Steinmetz noted that "the stress, frustration, and feelings of burden experienced by caregivers who are caring for dependent elders can result in abusive and neglectful treatment." In support of this statement, it has been shown that the more stressful the caregiving is *perceived* to be by middle-aged adults, the more likely they are to resort to using abusive behaviors against the elder. Furthermore [T.] Fulmer and [T.A.] O'Malley found that in comparison to 147 elders who were not referred for elder abuse, those 107 who were referred were more dependent on their caregivers.

Adult Dependent Child Hypothesis

Proponents of the view that elder abuse is primarily committed by adult dependent children relying on their aging parents for help rather than by adult caregivers taking care of elderly parents point to the fact that the majority of case control studies on this issue have found that victims of elder abuse do *not* differ from nonvictims in their health status and level of dependency. In addition, although women tend to be the primary caretakers of the elderly, males are more likely than females to perpetrate elder abuse, which points towards a weakness in the caretaker stress hypothesis. Pillemer argued that the popular assumption that elders are abused by their middle-aged, stronger caregivers stems from media attention and the attention of public officials. Indeed, we seem to be swayed morally by the notion that frail elders should be protected from the frustrations of their caregiving relatives. . . . [T]he majority of elder abuse intervention programs seem to be designed to reduce the stress of caregivers. But, as Pillemer argued, the more rigorous studies of elder abuse clearly show that we need to look at the characteristics of the abuser, not the characteristics of the victim, if we are to clearly understand elder abuse.

Research on characteristics of the abusers shows that typically they are the ones who are dependent. For example, in a survey of community agencies in Massachusetts, two thirds of the elder abuse cases were characterized by the adult child being financially dependent upon the abused elder. Of reported cases of elder abuse in Wisconsin, 75% of the abusers were living in the elder's home, and 25% were financially dependent upon the elder. Pillemer's own research also supports his supposition that elder abuse is committed by adult dependent children. In a series of studies, he found that in comparison to nonvictimized elders, those elders who were abused were more likely to have their adult children dependent upon them in several areas, including housing, household repair, financial assistance, transportation, and cooking and cleaning.

Poor Elderly More Likely to Be Abused

The NEAIS of 1996 reported predictors and correlates of elder abuse separately for cases reported by APS and by the sentinels [agencies who regularly work with the elderly]. The APS reports contained data on the income level, ethnicity, gender, age, and physical and mental frailty of the victims, and the sentinel reports had data on all of those variables except ethnicity and income. Furthermore, APS and sentinel reports contained data concerning the perpetrator's gender, age, race/ethnicity, and relationship to the victim. Many of the smaller-scale studies on elder abuse also provide data on predictors and correlates. Following is a summary of the findings of these reports and their similarities and differences. . . .

Abuse reported by APS in the NEAIS was most likely to have been perpetrated against older individuals earning under $15,000 per year. Specifically, in 91.5% of neglect cases, 75% of emotional/psychological abuse cases, 75.5% of physical abuse cases, 77.6% of financial exploitation cases, and 100% of abandonment cases, the victims made under $15,000. Also according to APS reports, the majority of the victims were White (84%), followed by Blacks (8.3%), Hispanics (5.1%), Asians (2.1%), and Native American Indians (0.4%). Whites were overrepresented in every category of abuse, with the exception of abandonment, in which a slight majority of victims (57.3%) were Black. The ethnicity of the perpetrators reflected that of the victims: The majority were White, according to both APS (77%) and sentinel (63.5%) reports.

Types of Elder Domestic Violence

"Domestic violence grown old" is when domestic violence started earlier in life and persists into old age.

"Late onset domestic violence" begins in old age. There may have been a strained relationship or emotional abuse earlier that got worse as the partners aged. When abuse begins or is exacerbated in old age, it is likely to be linked to:

- Retirement

- Disability

- Changing roles of family members

- Sexual changes

Some older people enter into abusive relationships late in life.

www.preventelderabuse.org

Frailty of the Victim

Researchers who assert that elder abuse is committed primarily by overstressed caretaking relatives tend to focus on the characteristics of the victims that predispose them to be at risk for abuse. For example, in a Wisconsin sample of 204 elder abuse cases, 51% of the victims were frail, 12% had Alzheimer's, and 20% were homebound. In comparison to the Wisconsin elderly population in general, in which 20% shared a household with someone other than a spouse, 73% of the abused elders lived with an adult child (75%, however, lived in the elder's home, not the child's home). In these cases, the frailty and incapacities of the elder are viewed as the factors that put them at risk for abuse by their caregiver relatives.

The NEAIS also provides evidence that frailty in elderly people may put them at risk for abuse. According to APS reports, the majority of elder abuse victims are unable (47.9%) or somewhat unable (28.7%) to care for themselves and sometimes confused (27.9%) or very confused and disoriented (31.6%). However, these statistics stand in stark contrast to those characterizing cases reported by sentinels: Only 18.8% were unable to care for themselves, 33.1% were somewhat able to, 7.5% were very confused and disoriented, and 37.9% were somewhat confused. Thus, the cases that were not necessarily reported to APS were ones where the elders showed higher functioning. . . .

Gender and Age of the Victim

According to both APS and sentinel reports of the NEAIS, elderly females were more likely to be abused than elderly males, even after accounting for elderly females' overrepresentation in the population. This was the case for every type of abuse reported to APS except for abandonment, in which males were more likely to be victimized. According to APS reports, the majority of reported elder abuse incidents were perpetrated against the oldest old—those who were aged 80 or older—and continually decreased as the age of the victim decreased. This pattern held true for elder abuse overall and for neglect, emotional abuse, physical abuse, and financial exploitation. (Sexual abuse and abandonment occurred too infrequently for exact rates by age to be estimated.) A different picture emerged for elder abuse cases reported by sentinels: Those who were aged 60–70 were the most likely to suffer from physical abuse, emotional abuse, neglect, and self-neglect. Those aged 71–80 were the most likely to suffer from abandonment, and those over age 80 were the most likely to be neglected.

Characteristics of Abusers

Researchers who stress that it is the dependency of the abuser on the elder—not the other way around—that contributes most to elder abuse tend to concentrate most on characteristics of the abuser (i.e., on individual/developmental level factors) that predict elder abuse. These predictors seem to mirror the most powerful predictors found for child and spousal abuse. For example, the abusers may have been subjected to abuse themselves when they were children, often by the elderly parent they are now abusing. Abusers are also likely to have problems with drugs and alcohol and may also have chronic psychological problems. Furthermore, abusers are likely to have mental and emotional problems, be hospitalized for those problems, and be violent and possibly arrested in other situations. Finally, in comparison to families not characterized by elder abuse, those experiencing elder abuse are more likely to have a family member with emotional problems and interpersonal difficulties and to be more socially isolated.

The NEAIS also provides data on individual/developmental level characteristics of the abusers. According to both APS and sentinel reports, the majority of abusers were male (53% and 63.1%, respectively). According to APS reports, males were more likely to commit every type of abuse except neglect. (Sentinel reports were not broken down by abuse type.) Also according to both APS and sentinel reports, the majority of abusers were under the age of 60 (66% and 60.7%, respectively), and, according to APS reports, individuals under 60 committed the majority of all types of abuse. Finally, according to both APS and sentinel reports, children were the most likely perpetrators of elder abuse (47% and 30.8%, respectively), followed by spouses (19% and 30.3%). Other perpetrators included parents, grandchildren, siblings, friends and neighbors, and other relatives, the relative distribution of which depended upon the agency reporting. . . .

Elders Don't Seek Help

[A] situation in which the victim of elder abuse is unwilling to be proactive in eliminating the violence in his/her life is not uncommon. Researchers in the field of elder abuse point to several reasons why elders are sometimes unwilling to take the necessary steps to free themselves from abuse. For instance, in the case of spousal abuse, they may have just given up on the idea of living a life that is free of maltreatment. There may also be a belief, which is particularly strong among the elderly, that it is inappropriate to share the secrets of the abusive behavior with strangers or even friends. There are also concerns for elderly victims [that if] their abusers were removed from the home, then there is the possibility that the elders would be isolated and no one would be there to help with transportation, finances, or chores. Finally, there is a reluctance to turn in a loved one, a reluctance that seems to be more pronounced when the abuser is a child rather than a spouse.

Periodical Bibliography

The following articles have been selected to supplement the diverse views in this chapter:

Jane Black — "The Not-So-Golden Years: Power of Attorney, Elder Abuse, and Why Our Laws Are Failing a Vulnerable Population," *St. John's Law Review*, Winter 2008.

F. Stephen Bridges, Kimberly M. Tatum, and Julie C. Kunselman — "Domestic Violence Statutes and Rates of Intimate Partner and Family Homicide," *Criminal Justice Policy Review*, March 2008.

Gene Feder — "Mandatory Reporting of Domestic Violence," *Lancet*, March 22, 2008.

Christine A. Helfrich, Glenn T. Fujiura, and Violet Rutkowski-Kmitta — "Mental Health Disorders and Functioning of Women in Domestic Violence Shelters," *Journal of Interpersonal Violence*, April 2008.

W.C. Holmes and M.D. Sammel — "Boys Are Victims of Domestic Violence," *Annals of Internal Medicine*, December 10, 2005, Vol. 143, Issue 8.

Heather Kettrey and Beth Emery — "The Discourse of Sibling Violence," *Journal of Family Violence*, November 2007, Vol. 22, Issue 8.

Erin L. Nabors, Tracy L. Dietz, and Jana L. Jasinski — "Children's Direct Sensory Exposure to Substantiated Domestic Violence Crimes," *Violence and Victims*, December 1, 2006.

Rebecca O'Reilly — "Domestic Violence Against Women in Their Childbearing Years: A Review of the Literature," *Contemporary Nurse*, May 1, 2007.

Kathryn M. Yount and Jennifer S. Carerra — "Domestic Violence Against Married Women in Cambodia," *Social Forces*, September 1, 2006.

OPPOSING
VIEWPOINTS®
SERIES

CHAPTER 2

Who Is Responsible for Domestic Violence?

Chapter Preface

The debate concerning domestic violence culpability is often a political one. As the issue of domestic violence has received more attention by the media, rival advocacy groups have increasingly appealed to state and federal legislators. Not surprisingly, the debate is drawn largely along gender lines. Many women's rights groups argue that men overwhelmingly instigate and perpetrate domestic violence. Some men's groups, however, maintain that women are the aggressors just as often, if not more often, in cases of domestic violence and that laws are unfairly stacked against men. Both groups cite research and studies to validate their claims.

The feminist perspective dominates much of the argument for men being the aggressors. According to the *National Journal*, the feminist position centers on the premise that men seek "to control their wives and girlfriends." This premise draws on years of historical and anecdotal evidence that some men attempt to "maintain patriarchal dominance" over women through physical and emotional abuse. According to Liz Cascone, from the Virginia Sexual and Domestic Violence Action Alliance, "There are larger cultural norms and attitudes around violence in relationships, and particularly violence against women, that come from our culture and years of socialization."

The alternative perspective, which is relatively new, is often referred to as the "family-conflict perspective." According to the *National Journal*, this viewpoint argues that "many cases of lesser violence emerge from routine family disagreements and should not be handled through the criminal justice system." While recognizing that some situations do require the legal system to step in, proponents of this perspective maintain that routine disagreements over such issues as finances or sex are often at the root of disputes and that financial assistance or education and therapy are more appropriate than jail time for abusers.

Advocates of the family-conflict perspective cite a 2007 study published by the *American Journal of Public Health* to show that "fifty percent of violent relationships included reciprocal pushing, hitting, and threats" and that "women made seven out of 10 attacks." Proponents of the feminist perspective, on the other hand, defend "FBI statistics [that] show that women are killed by intimate partners more than three times as often as men are."

The authors in this chapter utilize statistics and diverse reasoning in attempts to determine who is responsible for domestic violence.

"The purpose of domestic violence is to establish and exert power and control over another; men most often use it against their intimate partners."

Men's Desire to Control Women Is Responsible for Domestic Violence

Minnesota Advocates for Human Rights

In the following viewpoint, Minnesota Advocates for Human Rights (MAHR) argues that domestic violence is a tactic that men use to control women. Domestic violence, contends MAHR, occurs in part because society upholds the view that men have a right to control women by using force. According to MAHR, domestic violence can include physical assault, emotionally abusive behavior, or both. MAHR asserts that domestic violence is not rooted in mental illness or learned behaviors but is a product of the historically unequal relationships between men and women. Minnesota Advocates for Human Rights provides investigative fact finding, direct legal representation, collaboration for education and training, and publications concerning human rights.

Minnesota Advocates for Human Rights, "What Is Domestic Violence?" at Stop Violence Against Women: A project by The Advocates for Human Rights, 2003. www.stopvaw.org. Reproduced by permission.

As you read, consider the following questions:

1. Why, in the view of MAHR, is domestic violence repeated?
2. What is the flaw in the "learned helplessness" theory of domestic violence, according to the author?
3. According to research cited by MAHR, how many times must domestic violence occur before the abuser establishes control over the victim?

Domestic violence is a pattern of abusive and threatening behaviors that may include physical, emotional, economic and sexual violence as well as intimidation, isolation and coercion. The purpose of domestic violence is to establish and exert power and control over another; men most often use it against their intimate partners, which can include current or former spouses, girlfriends, or dating partners. While other forms of violence within the family are also serious, this [viewpoint] will address the unique characteristics of violence against women in their intimate relationships.

Society Sanctions Men's Control

Domestic violence is behavior that is learned through observation and reinforcement in both the family and society. It is not caused by genetics or illness. Domestic violence is repeated because it works. The pattern of domestic violence allows the perpetrator to gain control of the victim through fear and intimidation. Gaining the victim's compliance, even temporarily, reinforces the perpetrator's use of these tactics of control. More importantly, however, the perpetrator is able to reinforce his abusive behavior because of the socially sanctioned belief that men have the right to control women in relationships and the right to use force to ensure that control. . . .

Not a Mental Illness Issue

To be effective, intervention strategies for domestic violence must be based on a clearly articulated theory of violence. To the extent possible, all parts of the community must share this view of violence to effectively coordinate their responses to the problem.

Information regarding the evolution of theories of violence in the United States is useful because various forms of these theories are being discussed in many countries in Central and Eastern Europe and the Commonwealth of Independent States (CEE/CIS). The first theory developed in the United States was that men who battered women were mentally ill and that women who remained in violent relationships were also mentally ill. This theory proved to be wrong. The number of relationships that involved violence was much greater than original theorists guessed and psychological tests did not support the theory that violence was caused by mental illness. In fact, many batterers and their victims tested "normal" under psychological tests.

Not "Learned" Behavior

Another theory developed that men battered because they learned this behavior in their families. Although there is a statistical relationship between boys who witness their fathers battering their mothers (they are seven times more likely to batter their own wives), there is no significant statistical relationship between girls who witness battering and those who later become victims. Further, many men who witnessed violence as children do not abuse their partners as adults.

A third theory was that women suffered from a "learned helplessness" as a result of repeated battering, which prevented them from resisting the violence or leaving the relationship. This theory does not address the economic, social, and familial reasons that force women to stay in the relationship; it is also inconsistent with the experiences of many women who actively attempt to secure their safety. Research indicates that battered women resist the abuse in many ways and engage in a variety of survival or coping strategies.

Goal of Domestic Violence Is Control

Domestic violence is purposeful and instrumental behavior. The pattern of abuse is directed at achieving compliance from and control over the victim. It is directed at circumscribing the life of the victim so that independent thought and action are eliminated and so that the victim will become exclusively devoted to fulfilling the needs and requirements of the batterer. The pattern is not impulsive or out of control behavior. The batterer selectively chooses tactics that work to control the victim.

Some of the acts may appear to be directed against or involve children, property, or pets when in fact the batterer is engaging in these behaviors in order to control or punish the intimate partner (for example, physical attacks against a child, throwing furniture through a picture window, strangling the victim's pet cat, etc.). Although someone or something other than the victim is physically damaged, that particular assault is part of the pattern of abuse directed at the victim.

Kathy Scaggs, "Legal Advocacy for Victims of Domestic Violence,"
Tennessee Coalition Against Domestic Violence, August 2006.

No "Cycle of Violence"

Yet a fourth theory was that batterers follow a "cycle of violence" with intermittent violent and repentant episodes. The "cycle of violence" theory did not conform to many battered women's experiences. Many women reported that their partners never repented in their violent relationships, and that violence was not cyclical but rather a constant presence in their lives.

These theories evolved into the current understanding of why violence against women happens. This understanding of how and why men batter was developed through many years of interviews with victims and batterers. According to this model, batterers use abusive and threatening behaviors to exert and maintain control and power over their victims.

Male Oppression of Women

Although there are no simple explanations, research indicates that domestic violence has its roots in the subordinate role women have traditionally held in private and public life in many societies. The United Nations Declaration on the Elimination of Violence Against Women describes violence against women as "a manifestation of historically unequal power relationships between men and women." At the same time, violence is used to perpetuate and enforce women's subordinate role. In the Declaration on the Elimination of Violence Against Women, the United Nations and its member countries denounce domestic violence as one of the "crucial social mechanisms by which women are forced into subordinate [positions] compared with men." . . .

Methods of Control

Batterers use a wide range of coercive and abusive behaviors against their victims. Some of the abusive behaviors used by batterers result in physical injuries that harm the victim both physically and emotionally. Other techniques employed by batterers involve emotionally abusive behaviors. While these behaviors may not result in physical injuries, they are still psychologically damaging to the victim. Batterers employ different abusive behaviors at different times. Even a single incident of physical violence may be sufficient to establish power and control over a partner; this power and control is then reinforced and strengthened by non-physical abusive and coercive behaviors.

I *"Wives are just as controlling as husbands."*

Men Who Commit Domestic Violence Are No More Controlling than Women

Maureen C. Outlaw and Richard B. Felson

In the following viewpoint, Maureen C. Outlaw and Richard B. Felson argue that domestic violence is not a function of men wanting to control women—that men are in fact not more controlling than women. Both genders are motivated to control, say the authors, but the methods of control may differ. While Outlaw and Felson do find some gender differences in the degree of control when comparing current marriages to former marriages, they maintain that controlling behaviors, rather than gender, correlates with domestic violence. Maureen C. Outlaw and Richard B. Felson are professors at Providence College and Pennsylvania State University, respectively.

As you read, consider the following questions:

1. According to the authors, who is more controlling and jealous in current marriages, the husband or the wife?

2. In Outlaw and Felson' view, how do the findings from their research affect the feminist theory of domestic violence?

3. According to the authors, what is the correlation between control and jealousy issues and the gender of those who commit domestic violence against former spouses?

The role of the control motive in marital violence is examined using data on current and former marriages from the Survey of Violence and Threats of Violence Against Women and Men. The findings indicate no support for the position that husbands engage in more marital violence than wives because they are more controlling. In former marriages, we observe statistical interactions between gender and control: former husbands who were controlling or jealous were particularly likely to be verbally aggressive and to engage in violence. The controlling husbands (present and former), however, are not particularly likely to engage in violence that is frequent, injurious, or unprovoked. The evidence suggests that husband and wives may differ in their methods of control but not their motivation to control. . . .

Gender Roles

The data provide no support for the hypothesis that men are more likely than women to use violence against their spouse because they are more controlling or jealous. In current marriages, wives are more controlling and jealous than husbands, while in former marriages, husbands are more controlling, but there is a significant difference in jealousy. Differences in control behavior and jealousy do not mediate the gender-violence relationship in marriage.

Gender differences in control behavior varied for different behaviors. They appeared to reflect gender roles and the stereotypical concerns of husbands and wives. Women spend more time in the home, so they are more likely to have strong opinions on where the couple lives. Men are more prone to infidelity, so women are more likely to attempt to control who their associates are. Men are expected to work outside the home, so women are less likely to attempt to prevent them from doing so. Finally, in troubled marriages, men are more likely to hide information on income, perhaps in anticipation of divorce.

Controlling Wives

In general, our results are consistent with those of [J.] Stets and [S.A.] Hammond in showing that wives are more controlling than husbands in their current marriages. We also found that wives are more likely to be jealous and possessive. The evidence does not support either feminist theory or evolutionary psychology since both predict a gender difference in the other direction. Two factors could lead to a higher incidence of control behavior and jealousy among wives. First, it may be that men's greater propensity for cheating and other misbehavior elicits more control behavior and jealousy from their wives. In other words, women may have more reason to be controlling and jealous than men. Second, gender differences in control behavior may reflect men's stoicism. Men are less active than women when they believe they have been wronged. Thus, research consistently shows that women are more likely than men to complain and to express anger in a nonaggressive way when they have a grievance. Complaints and expressions of anger are often attempts to influence the behavior of others. Note that gender differences in complaining are observed in experimental studies that hold provocation constant and in a wide variety of situations, not just those produced by their husbands. This evidence is consistent with the notion that husbands and wives differ in their method of control, not the

Women Wield the Power in Marriage

A study [by researchers at Iowa State University] of 72 married couples from Iowa found that wives, on average, exhibit greater situational power—in the form of domineering and dominant behaviors—than their husbands during problem-solving discussions, regardless of who raised the topic.

Rick Nauert, "Women Wield the Power in Marriage,"
July 6, 2007. http://psychcentral.com.

motive to control. Wives are just as controlling as husbands, but they are less likely to use violent means to achieve influence.

Angry Ex-husbands

In former marriages, there is strong and consistent evidence of statistical interactions involving gender. In these marriages, control behavior and jealousy are much more strongly related to aggression and violence for men than for women. The evidence supports the idea that, in troubled marriages, men and women differ in their methods of control rather than in their overall desire to control. The results do not support the idea that control behavior reflects the patriarchal ideology of men. This conclusion obviously requires some inferences, but we cannot imagine other explanations for the strong patterns we observe. It should be noted that past research is mixed as to whether men with traditional attitudes toward gender roles are more likely than men with liberal attitudes to commit marital violence.

Although there are some interactions with gender, the evidence is clear that control behavior and jealousy are strong predictors of aggression for both men and women. This research, therefore, supports the idea that control and jealousy motives lead to spousal violence. It is also likely, however, that these relationships are at least partly spurious. For example, if a marriage is troubled, people may mistreat their spouses in a variety of ways, that is, with verbal aggression, controlling behavior, violence, and infidelity.

Controlling Behaviors, Not Gender, Is Key

[M.] Johnson's distinction between intimate terrorism and common couple violence has been influential in part because it provides a compromise between feminist and domestic violence researchers. However, it has never been subjected to an adequate empirical test. The key hypothesis derived from his typology is that controlling husbands are particularly likely to engage in more serious forms of violence. Our evidence does not support this hypothesis. Controlling and jealous husbands are not particularly likely to engage in violence that is frequent, injurious, or unprovoked by a physical attack.

We do find evidence for main effects of controlling behavior and jealousy on the likelihood of injurious violence and on the frequency of violence. Both husbands and wives who are controlling are more likely to produce injury and engage in repeated violence. Similar effects are observed for jealousy, although not all are statistically significant. The seriousness of violence is apparently associated with motive, although the relationship does not depend on gender. The relationship, however, could be spurious because of some unmeasured characteristic of individuals or the quality of marriages. For example, spouses may be more controlling and jealous and commit frequent violence in marriages with infidelity and other conflicts. . . .

Gender Affects Method of Control

It may be that typologies, in general, exaggerate the differences between different types of offenders. For example, even if control behavior could be shown to be related to the severity and frequency of husbands' violence, the relationships are not likely to be strong. One might argue that they are not strong enough to justify a typology that treats violent, controlling spouses as qualitatively different from other violent spouses. In addition, the use of the emotionally charged word "terrorist" to describe these men and women may be misleading.

In sum, this research suggests that control behavior and jealousy play a role in violence in current marriages, but they cannot explain gender differences. In marriages that end in divorce, on the other hand, husbands are more violent than wives, and controlling husbands are particularly violent. However, even in these troubled marriages, gender appears to be related to method of control, not motive for control.

> "[There is] an epidemic of women who pummel their husbands and boy-friends."

Women Are Responsible for More Domestic Violence than Are Men

Carey Roberts

In the following viewpoint, Carey Roberts argues that research shows that women are responsible for more domestic violence than men are. The author notes as well that women not only feel no shame about committing domestic violence, they often brag about beating up husbands and boyfriends. The attitude of women regarding their own domestic violence, he contends, belies the view that women are less aggressive than men. Carey Roberts is an analyst and commentator on political correctness.

As you read, consider the following questions:

1. According to a study cited by the author, what percentage of nonreciprocal partner violence is instigated by women?

2. What superstar is quoted by Roberts as admitting that she beats up her husband when she's drunk?

3. Among women interviewed by the author, what is the most common justification for committing domestic violence against men?

Chivalrous men resist the image, but it's a problem that has become so pervasive that we must summon up the courage to face it—an epidemic of women who pummel their husbands and boyfriends.

A recent survey by the Centers for Disease Control found that among physically aggressive couples, 71% of the instigators in nonreciprocal partner violence were female. And [in 2006] Renee McDonald of Baylor University published a study in the *Journal of Family Psychology* with almost identical results.

What's going on, ladies?

Women Abusing Men

The problem isn't just gals who clean their boyfriends' clock in a drunken rage. These high-testosterone females abuse their men and then come clean with a swaggering braggadocio.

A few months ago ABC *Primetime* did an experiment. The producers hired two actors—male and female—to feign partner violence in a public park. They wanted to see what passers-by would do when they spotted the woman pounding her boyfriend with a rolled-up newspaper. . . .

Most persons paused, then cast a "it's not my problem" shrug. But one young lass was caught on camera doing a pumped-fist "atta-woman" salute. You go, girl!

That would never happen in real life, right?

Consider superstar singer Amy Winehouse. Married to Blake Fielder-Civil, she now admits that she uses him as a "punch-bag." "I'll beat up Blake when I'm drunk. . . . If he says one thing I don't like then I'll chin him," she brags.

College Women Abuse College Men

[Murray] Straus, co-director of the Family Research Lab at the University of New Hampshire, recently completed an international study on partner violence among university students. His queries of more than 13,600 students revealed that the most common instance of partner violence is mutual abuse.

The second most common situation of partner violence is when the female is the perpetrator against the male, he said. This leaves the reverse—when males abuse females—to be the least common in practice, although the most common in publicity.

www.fosters.com, July 5, 2006.

I recently came across a website called Jezebel.com. Jezebel is one of those tell-all websites run by women who flaunt tattoos that declare, "I know what I want and I know how to get it."

Female Empowerment?

Recently a Jezebel editor named Slut Machine posted a cheeky piece called, "Have You Ever Beat Up a Boyfriend? Cause, Uh, We Have." Let's put it this way—the column brings a whole new meaning to the phrase, "female empowerment."

Ms. Machine confided that one of her co-editors had overheard her boyfriend flirting on the phone, "so she slapped the phone out of his hands and hit him in the face and neck." Another smacked a guy when he tenderly revealed to her "he thought he had breast cancer." As an afterthought she wrote, "that one made us laugh really hard."

I was certain that such brazen admissions would draw howls of protest from persons who know full well that "there's no excuse for domestic violence." Well, this is what they said:

Probationer announced to her on-line Sisterhood, "Yeah, I've punched the shit out of a guy. But I don't like to brag."

Fromthetulleshed bragged, "I've had many satisfying dreams where I beat up my ex."

"If I saw him again, I don't think I'd be able to restrain myself."

Some thought assaulting a guy was downright hilarious: "I bounced an alarm clock off my husband's head from across the room once. I haven't been able to find a decent alarm clock since," lamented Kwindsorfish.

Varied Forms of Abuse

And Sparkle proved you don't have to be physical to be abusive: "I try so so SO hard to do the sitting silently trick. . . . But I just couldn't keep myself from laughing after like a minute thirty of 'ignoring' him. It just makes me too giddy to think that I can have that much power by doing absolutely nothing at all."

When it came to the fact that female abusers often use weapons or the element of surprise to compensate for their smaller size, the women seemed clueless. JoanCrawford revealed, "My Ex told me his former lover beat him. I was a bit startled when I met her. He is 6'3" about 195 lbs.; she was 5' and appeared to weigh literally 98 lbs. Battered men? The question is, are these men really physically afraid?"

Creative excuses were *de rigueur*. Goupie reasoned, "I slap my boyfriend on a semi-regular basis. It always hurts me more than it hurts him. And he usually agrees that he deserves it." Azi's comment, "I have to say I think he may have had it coming," was the most common pretext.

And Crocodile Tears of remorse were shed by the bucketfull. Washionfore confessed, "I have slapped a man down before, quite hard, but I love him so I felt bad because, well, it's abusive."

Actress Sally Field recently received an Emmy Award for best actress. During her acceptance speech she boasted that women are of the peace-loving kind, crudely shouting, "And, let's face it, if the mothers ruled the world, there would be no [expletive deleted] wars in the first place."

But based on the gleeful comments of the naughty Jezebel girls, somehow I don't think Miss Field's act is ready for prime time.

*"The prevalence of domestic violence in
a given society . . . is the result of tacit
acceptance by that society."*

Society Reinforces Violence Against Women

United Nations Population Fund

*In the following viewpoint, the United Nations Population Fund
(UNFPA) argues that domestic violence against women is caused
by gender inequality. Gender roles are unequal, UNFPA contends, and domestic violence is a method for perpetuating that
inequality. The organization claims that women are subject to
domestic violence from birth to old age, and that society reinforces domestic violence by its acceptance of it. Only if the problem is publicized and women speak out can gender-based violence be reduced. UNFPA is an international development agency
that supports countries in using population data for policies and
programs that reduce poverty and improve the lives of women,
men and children around the world.*

As you read, consider the following questions:

1. According to sources cited by UNFPA, what is the most
   pervasive yet least recognized human rights abuse in the
   world?

2. How, in the view of the author, is gender violence perpetrated in the prenatal stage of a woman's life?

3. What culture-based concepts must be changed, according to UNFPA, to end gender-based violence?

Around the world, as many as one in every three women has been beaten, coerced into sex, or abused in some other way—most often by someone she knows, including by her husband or another male family member; one woman in four has been abused during pregnancy.

> "Violence against women both violates and impairs or nullifies the enjoyment by women of their human rights and fundamental freedoms.... In all societies, to a greater or lesser degree, women and girls are subjected to physical, sexual and psychological abuse that cuts across lines of income, class and culture." —Beijing Declaration and Platform for Action

Gender-Based Violence and Inequality

Gender-based violence both reflects and reinforces inequities between men and women and compromises the health, dignity, security and autonomy of its victims. It encompasses a wide range of human rights violations, including sexual abuse of children, rape, domestic violence, sexual assault and harassment, trafficking of women and girls and several harmful traditional practices. Any one of these abuses can leave deep psychological scars, damage the health of women and girls in general, including their reproductive and sexual health, and in some instances, results in death.

Violence against women has been called "the most pervasive yet least recognized human rights abuse in the world." Accordingly, the Vienna Human Rights Conference and the Fourth World Conference on Women gave priority to this issue, which jeopardizes women's lives, bodies, psychological integrity and freedom. Violence may have profound effects—direct and indirect—on a woman's reproductive health, including:

- Unwanted pregnancies and restricted access to family planning information and contraceptives

- Unsafe abortion or injuries sustained during a legal abortion after an unwanted pregnancy

- Complications from frequent, high-risk pregnancies and lack of follow-up care

- Sexually transmitted infections, including HIV/AIDS

- Persistent gynaecological problems

- Psychological problems

Violence Perpetuates Male Power

Gender-based violence also serves—by intention or effect—to perpetuate male power and control. It is sustained by a culture of silence and denial of the seriousness of the health consequences of abuse. In addition to the harm they exact on the individual level, these consequences also exact a social toll and place a heavy and unnecessary burden on health services.

UNFPA [United Nations Population Fund] recognizes that violence against women is inextricably linked to gender-based inequalities. When women and girls are expected to be generally subservient, their behaviour in relation to their health, including reproductive health, is negatively affected at all stages of the life cycle.

UNFPA puts every effort into breaking the silence and ensuring that the voices of women are heard. At the same time, the Fund works to change the paradigm of masculinity that allows for the resolution of conflict through violence. One strategy is to engage men—policy makers, parents and young boys—in discourse about the dynamics and consequences of violence.

A Lifetime of Domestic Violence

As the [list] below shows, women may face different forms of violence at different stages of their lives.

Gender Violence Throughout a Woman's Life

- Prenatal: Prenatal sex selection, battering during pregnancy, coerced pregnancy (rape during war)

- Infancy: Female infanticide, emotional and physical abuse, differential access to food and medical care

- Childhood: Genital cutting; incest and sexual abuse; differential access to food, medical care, and education; child prostitution

- Adolescence: Dating and courtship violence, economically coerced sex, sexual abuse in the workplace, rape, sexual harassment, forced prostitution

- Reproductive: Abuse of women by intimate partners, marital rape, dowry abuse and murders, partner homicide, psychological abuse, sexual abuse in the workplace, sexual harassment, rape, abuse of women with disabilities

- Old Age: Abuse of widows, elder abuse (which affects mostly women)

Violence at Home

Most domestic violence involves male anger directed against their women partners. This gender difference appears to be rooted in the way boys and men are socialized—biological factors do not seem to account for the dramatic differences in behaviour in this regard between men and women.

Pregnant women are particularly vulnerable to gender-based violence. Some husbands become more violent during

Society Sanctions Power over Women

When I say that domestic violence is gender based, I am not referring to the fact that domestic violence is generally committed by persons of one sex against those of the other. Instead, I am referring to the *gendered underpinnings* of such violence. Gender is the socially constructed dimension of biologically determined sex. As such, gender encompasses the different roles, rights, and obligations ascribed by culture and society to women and men because of their sex. These ascribed roles, rights, and obligations are not just different, they also tend to be unequal: Men have more power than women do, and in some relationships, such as marriage, men may also have socially, culturally, or even legally sanctioned power *over* women.

Sunita Kishor, "The Heavy Burden of a Silent Scourge: Domestic Violence," Revista Panamericana de Salud Publica/ Pan American Journal of Public Health, *February 28, 2005.*

the wife's pregnancy, even kicking or hitting their wives in the belly. These women run twice the risk of miscarriage and four times the risk of having a low birth-weight baby.

Cross-cultural studies of wife abuse have found that nearly a fifth of peasant and small-scale societies are essentially free of family violence. The existence of such cultures proves that male violence against women is not the inevitable result of male biology or sexuality, but more a matter of how society views masculinity.

Society Reinforces Domestic Violence

Studies of very young boys and girls show only that, although boys may have a lower tolerance for frustration, and a tendency towards rough-and-tumble play, these tendencies are dwarfed by the importance of male socialization and peer pressure into gender roles.

The prevalence of domestic violence in a given society, therefore, is the result of tacit acceptance by that society. The way men view themselves as men, and the way they view women, will determine whether they use violence or coercion against women.

UNFPA recognizes that ending gender-based violence will mean changing cultural concepts about masculinity, and that process must actively engage men, whether they be policy makers, parents, spouses or young boys.

Sexual Assault

The majority of sexual assault victims are young. Women in positions of abject dependence on male authorities are also particularly subject to unwanted sexual coercion. Rape in time of war is still common. It has been extensively documented in recent civil conflicts, and has been used systematically as an instrument of torture or ethnic domination.

Now, with precedents set at the International Criminal Tribunal for Rwanda, in Tanzania, and the International Criminal Tribunal for the Former Yugoslavia, at The Hague, for mass rape, other acts such as sexual assault, sexual slavery, forced prostitution, forced sterilization, forced abortion, and forced pregnancy may qualify as crimes of torture, crimes against humanity, and even some as crimes of genocide.

Women Must Speak Out

Because gender-based violence is sustained by silence, women's voices must be heard. UNFPA puts every effort into enabling women to speak out against gender-based violence, and to get help when they are victims of it. The Fund is also committed to keeping gender-based violence in the spotlight as a major health and human rights concern.

UNFPA advocates for legislative reform and enforcement of laws for the promotion and the protection of women's rights to reproductive health choices and informed consent, including promotion of women's awareness of laws, regulations and policies that affect their rights and responsibilities in family life. The Fund promotes zero tolerance of all forms of violence against women and works for the eradication of traditional practices that are harmful to women's reproductive and sexual health, such as rituals associated with puberty.

Periodical Bibliography

The following articles have been selected to supplement the diverse views in this chapter:

Lyn Mikel Brown, Meda Chesney-Lind, and Nan Stein	"Patriarchy Matters," *Violence Against Women*, December 2007.
Michelle Madden Dempsey	"Toward a Feminist State: What Does 'Effective' Prosecution of Domestic Violence Mean?" *Modern Law Review*, November 2007.
Miriam K. Ehrensaft	"Intimate Partner Violence: Persistence of Myths and Implications for Intervention," *Children & Youth Services Review*, March 2008.
Estelle Freedman	"Patriarchy Revisited: Gender, Race, and Sexual Violence," *Journal of Women's History*, Winter 2007.
Kathleen K. Furniss	"Ending the Cycle of Abuse: What Behavioral Health Professionals Need to Know About Domestic Violence," *Behavioral Healthcare*, February 1, 2006.
Peggy Grauwiler	"Voices of Women: Perspectives on Decision-Making and the Management of Partner Violence," *Children & Youth Services Review*, March 2008.
William F. McKibbin, Todd K. Shackelford, and Aaron T. Goetz	"Why Do Men Rape? An Evolutionary Psychological Perspective," *Review of General Psychology*, March 2008.
Merry Morash, Bui Hoan, Zhang Yan, and Kristy Holtfreter	"Risk Factors for Abusive Relationships," *Violence Against Women*, July 2007.
Deborah M. Weissman	"The Personal Is Political—and Economic: Rethinking Domestic Violence," *Brigham Young University Law Review*, vol. 2007, no. 2, 2007.

OPPOSING
VIEWPOINTS®
SERIES

CHAPTER 3

Is the Law Effective in Dealing with Domestic Violence?

Chapter Preface

Author Margaret C. Jasper, in *The Law of Violence Against Women*, notes that "historically, domestic violence was often viewed as a private family matter. Law enforcement often took the position that domestic violence was not a criminal offense." Jasper points out that the victim was often blamed for provoking the abuse and, as a result, "frequently remained silent about the abuse, rather than suffer criticism and shame, and possible retaliation by the abuser for involving the police."

During the 1970s, feminists and other groups argued that domestic violence was not merely a private family matter but a serious problem that should be addressed by the legal system; however, as Billie Lee Dunford-Jackson, Loretta Frederick, Barbara Hart, and Meredith Hofford point out in *Unified Family Courts: How Will They Service Victims of Domestic Violence?*, domestic violence presents special problems for the court system. Unlike other types of domestic issues, violence is difficult to resolve in a way satisfactory to all parties. Alternative dispute resolution processes, such as mediation, can be manipulated by the abuser. Attempts to preserve the family unit—often a noble goal in other types of disputes—may put victims and their children in danger and prolong subjugation to the abuser.

The rise in awareness of domestic violence as a legal problem led to the passage of the Violence Against Women's Act (VAWA) in 1994. The VAWA, says Jasper, is "landmark bipartisan legislation which sets forth firm law enforcement tactics and includes important safeguards for female victims of domestic violence and sexual assault." The Battered Women's Legal Advocacy Project claims that "VAWA has revolutionized the way that the legal system responds to violence against women through training of police, prosecutors, and court officials." According to New York Attorney General Andrew

Cuomo, VAWA has proven to be "successful and crucial programming that has reduced the incidence of violence against women, teens, and young adults."

However, not everyone agrees that VAWA has been a success. One advocacy group particularly critical of VAWA is Respecting Accuracy in Domestic Abuse Reportings (RADAR). RADAR claims that "VAWA-funded programs have brought about widespread civil rights violations, including problems with sex discrimination, denial of due process, and disregard of the presumption of innocence."

One objection critics make of VAWA is that it presumes that women, not men, are the victims of domestic violence and, consequently, the programs it funds reflect bias towards women. RADAR says men are the recipients of domestic violence as often as women are, and that the number of cases in which both the woman and the man are violent to each other is equal to the number of female pure victims and the number of male pure victims put together. But VAWA-funded programs serve male victims poorly or not at all, and they deny the existence of mutual violence. Another objection critics make is that the reauthorized version of VAWA enacted in 2000 promoted mandatory arrest laws. According to RADAR, a recent analysis from Harvard University shows that mandatory arrest laws actually increased intimate partner homicides by 60 percent rather than reduce subsequent incidents of domestic violence.

However, the federal Bureau of Justice Statistics has recently shown that intimate couple violence is at an all-time low, which may be proof that VAWA is working. Not only has non-lethal violence against women declined, but fatal violence against men has also declined dramatically. According to Richard Gelles, dean of the University of Pennsylvania's School of Social Policy and Practice, "We've eliminated a great deal of defensive homicide by giving women easier access to shelters and ERs and by measures such as mandatory arrest laws."

The viewpoints in this chapter take up the debate of safety and justice factors, as they relate to legal involvement in domestic violence.

> *"The Violence Against Women Act ...
> has provided federal grants to help
> communities across America develop
> innovative strategies to respond to vio-
> lence against women."*

The Violence Against Women Act Is Effective

Diane M. Stuart

In the following viewpoint, Diane M. Stuart argues that grants provided through the Violence Against Women Act (VAWA) are helping communities nationwide. Citing data provided by grant-ees, she states that VAWA has been effective in addressing domestic violence through direct services to victims, training for those who help them, and research. VAWA not only funds training of judges, she notes, but also provides prosecutors with tools to bring abusers to justice. This viewpoint is taken from Senate testimony given by Stuart when she was director of the Office on Violence Against Women in the U.S. Department of Justice.

As you read, consider the following questions:

1. According to figures cited by the author, how do the number of domestic violence grants awarded from 1997 to 2000 compare with the number awarded from 2001 to 2004?

Diane M. Stuart, "Testimony Before the Committee on the Judiciary, United States Senate, Concerning Reauthorization of the Violence Against Women Act," July 19, 2005.

2. What law required the U.S. attorney general to develop a protocol for sexual assault forensic examination, according to the Stuart?

3. According to figures cited by the author, how many federal indictments in domestic violence cases were filed by the Department of Justice in fiscal year 2004?

Almost 11 years ago, Congress passed VAWA [Violence Against Women Act]—landmark legislation in its scope and in its mission. Through new federal criminal provisions and important grant programs, we have been able to transform our nation's response to domestic violence, dating violence, sexual assault, and stalking. VAWA funds have supported the enforcement of protection orders, legal assistance, intensive training, community education, and local efforts to bring communities together to respond to violence against women.

Since the passage of VAWA, there has been a paradigm shift in how we approach and respond to violence against women. That change can be seen in local coordinated community responses. It is an approach rooted in the belief that criminal justice officials, victim advocates, community leaders, health workers, elected officials, and others must work in collaboration to respond to violence against women. . . .

Community Grants

OVW [the Office on Violence Against Women] was created in 1995 to implement VAWA and provide national leadership against domestic violence, dating violence, sexual assault, and stalking. OVW administers one formula grant program and eleven discretionary grant programs. . . .

Under grant programs established by VAWA, the Violence Against Women Act of 2000 (VAWA 2000), and other legislation, OVW has provided federal grants to help communities across America develop innovative strategies to respond to violence against women. These grant programs are being used to forge focused and effective partnerships among federal, state, local and tribal governments, and between the criminal justice system and victim advocates, and to provide much-needed services to victims of domestic violence, dating violence, sexual assault, and stalking.

New Programs

During [the George W. Bush] Administration, OVW has presided over an unprecedented expansion of its grant programs, both in terms of the types of services funded and the level of funding awarded. Since the beginning of FY [fiscal year] 2001, OVW has developed and implemented five new grant programs authorized under VAWA 2000. Funding under a sixth new program, which provides transitional housing assistance for victims of domestic violence, will be awarded for the first time in September, 2005. These programs have enabled communities to increase their efforts to help some of the most vulnerable victims, including the elderly and those with disabilities, and to provide supervised visitation services for victims and their children. In addition, through two of these new programs, OVW has supported the vital work that state sexual assault and domestic violence coalitions perform in each state and has fostered the growth of parallel coalitions in tribal communities. Due to statutory changes enacted in VAWA 2000, OVW also has been able to fund community work in new directions, such as help for immigrant victims of abuse and victims of dating violence, training for sexual assault forensic examiners, and improved enforcement of protection orders.

[From 2001 to 2005], increased funding for OVW programs also has allowed OVW to provide grants and technical assistance to more communities nationwide than ever before. During [the G.W. Bush] Administration, OVW has awarded nearly $1.25 billion in grants and cooperative agreements. During fiscal years 1997 through 2000, OVW made approximately 1500 such awards; during fiscal years 2001 through 2004, that number grew to nearly 2400. A new round of awards will be made during fiscal year 2005.

Native Women

Moreover, OVW has focused special attention on communities that face particularly acute challenges in responding to violence against women. For example, in June 2004, OVW convened a two-and-a-half-day summit on violence against women in Alaska. For the first time ever, tribal and state agencies in Alaska convened to discuss strengthening their response to sexual assault of Alaska Native women, who experience alarmingly high rates of sexual assault. Through the Safe Return Initiative, OVW funds community education, training, and on-site assistance to address domestic violence among prisoners leaving correctional facilities.

Measuring Effectiveness

[From 2002 to 2005], OVW has undertaken a significant effort to implement a system for measuring the effectiveness of projects supported by VAWA grant monies. Two Congressional mandates undergird this effort: a new reporting provision included in VAWA 2000, which requires OVW to prepare biennial reports to Congress that assess the effectiveness of projects supported with our funds, and the Government Performance and Results Act of 1993 (GPRA).

After an extensive process of consultation with OVW grantees and experts in the field, we have developed new progress reporting forms for grantees and subgrantees of OVW's grant programs. Each form is individualized to allow grantees to report on the types of activities—for example, training, criminal justice activities, victim services—they are engaged in with their grant funding.

Furthermore, the forms incorporate new GPRA measures to reflect more accurately the goals of OVW grant programs and whether those goals are being achieved. Data from the progress report forms can be used for individual project monitoring, feedback to grantees, and long-term planning, as well as reporting to Congress.

Positive Results

We are very excited about the data that grantees are submitting. For example, under one of our grant programs for just a six-month reporting period we know that:

- More than 50,000 victims were served;

- Over 120,000 services were provided to victims;

- Nearly 24,000 individuals were trained, including law enforcement, victim advocates, health professionals, court-based staff, and faith-based staff;

- 82 percent of cases received by courts resulted in charges being filed or transferred to a higher or lower court; and

- More than 2,600 individuals were arrested for violation of protection orders.

These numbers give us insight into the work of our grantees that we have never had before. . . .

Forensic Exam Protocol

Under the Violence Against Women Act of 2000, the Attorney General was required to develop a recommended national protocol, and establish a mechanism for its dissemination. As the entity within the Department of Justice tasked with developing the protocol, OVW consulted with national, state, tribal and local experts on rape/sexual assault, including rape crisis centers, domestic violence and sexual assault coalitions, and programs for criminal justice, forensic nursing, forensic science, emergency room medicine, law, social services, and sex crimes in underserved communities. The Protocol was released by the Attorney General in September, 2004.

The goals of the Protocol are to ensure that all victims, regardless of differences in background or location of service provision, receive the same high quality medical and forensic exam while being treated with respect and compassion and to improve prosecution of sexual assault cases through the appropriate collection of evidence. The Protocol is intended to supplement but not supersede prior developed protocols and support the use of the coordinated community response.

To enhance the utility of the Protocol, OVW is developing a technical assistance initiative to assist jurisdictions with its implementation. OVW has teamed with a forensic nurses organization to develop a centralized "clearinghouse" that will respond to requests from the field for assistance. Partner organizations representing law enforcement, prosecution, the tribal community, victim advocates and sexual assault coalitions, will contribute to the project....

Training Judges

Concerned that judicial training lagged behind other training efforts, OVW launched a significant effort to improve the ways in which courts respond to domestic violence. In 1998, OVW engaged in a cooperative agreement with the National Council of Juvenile and Family Court Judges (NCJFCJ), to develop the National Judicial Institute on Domestic Violence (Judicial Institute). In VAWA 2000, Congress further highlighted the critical role the courts play in responding to violence against women by making courts directly eligible for support under OVW's two largest grant programs. In fiscal year 2003, OVW expanded the reach of the Judicial Institute to include the breadth of judicial officers as well as to reach a greater number of courts and communities.

Through the Judicial Institute, NCJFCJ and its partner organization, the Family Violence Prevention Fund, created a

VAWA Overwhelmingly Approved

In June 2005, Congress introduced the *Violence Against Women Act (VAWA) of 2005*, bipartisan legislation to reauthorize the VAWA legislation originally passed in 1994. Since VAWA first became law in 1994, more than 660 state laws protecting victims of domestic violence and sexual assault have been passed, and VAWA 2005 has an even more comprehensive approach to the problem of violence.... The House passed VAWA with an overwhelming 415-4 vote for approval on September 8, followed by unanimous Senate approval on October 4. President [George W.] Bush signed the bill into law on January 5, 2006, continuing it for five more years.

National Research Center for Women and Families, April 2006. www.center4research.org/vawa2005.html.

highly interactive three-day seminar on domestic violence that is designed not only to impart needed information on such judicial practice areas as fact-finding and decision-making, but also to change judges' attitudes and values about domestic violence, victims, and perpetrators. Since 2000, more than 1,100 judges from all 50 states and the District of Columbia have been trained. Many of those judges indicated that the education received from the Institute was the best they have received on any topic, let alone domestic violence.

In addition to the judges trained at the three-day basic seminar, the Judicial Institute also has trained more than 130 judges in three-day seminars covering a range of issues including the overlap of domestic violence and child maltreatment, working with men who batter, and immigration. Other educational opportunities offered through the Judicial Institute have included training for more than 700 judges on such important domestic violence-related issues as firearms, evidence, and child custody, among others.

The Judicial Institute has done more than train judges; it has created a national community of judges leading the nation in responding to domestic violence. NCJFCJ regularly hear from professionals around the country that the work of the Judicial Institute has significantly improved judicial handling of domestic violence cases in their communities. In addition, OVW has replicated these Institutes for law enforcement and prosecutors.

Research on Violence Against Women

Research plays a vital role in determining the frequency of violent crimes against women, factors related to these crimes, and the impact of interventions designed to protect women and hold offenders accountable. Approximately $5 million of VAWA funding is provided annually to the National Institute of Justice (NIJ) to support research and evaluation efforts on issues related to violence against women.

This investment has yielded useful and practical results. Research on risk assessment instruments has shed light on the accuracy of different approaches to predicting risk of future harm or lethality in domestic violence cases. This research will have immediate use for advocates and others who work with domestic violence victims in developing effective safety plans and on how best to prevent or restrict further abusive behavior. VAWA-funded NIJ research, reported in the *Journal of the American Medical Association*, has determined the effectiveness of protection orders, concluding that permanent orders are associated with a significant decrease in risk of violence reported to police. Such results can give criminal justice officials greater confidence in granting permanent protection orders, when effectively enforced. VAWA-funded research has also addressed batterer intervention programs, seeking to determine whether or not they have an impact. While programs for batterers may not in themselves reduce domestic violence, we know that in a community with a coordinated approach to domestic violence and strong judicial oversight, these programs are a critical ingredient.

There have also been important research results on sexual violence. NIJ research has found that a sexual assault response team approach greatly enhances the quality of healthcare provided to women who have been sexually assaulted, improves the quality of forensic evidence, improves law enforcement's ability to collect information and to file charges, and increases the likelihood of successful prosecution. . . .

Criminal Prosecutions Under VAWA

In addition to ensuring services for victims, VAWA also strives to hold batterers, stalkers, and rapists accountable for their crimes. VAWA supplies federal prosecutors with important tools to combine efforts with state and local prosecutors in their work against domestic violence and stalking. VAWA and subsequent legislation created new federal interstate domestic violence, stalking and firearms crimes, strengthened federal penalties for repeat sex offenders, and required states and territories to enforce protection orders issued by other states, tribes and territories. United States Attorneys' Offices have formed partnerships with local law enforcement and prosecutors in a nationwide effort to end violence against women. Since the enactment of VAWA, the Justice Department has prosecuted more than 1,600 cases—cases with some of the most dangerous and determined abusers who have aggressively pursued their victims across state lines. In fiscal year 2004 alone, 324 indictments were filed, the highest amount since the enactment of the statutes. Prior to VAWA, many of these cases might have slipped through the cracks.

| *"VAWA-funded programs appear to be ineffective and sometimes harmful."*

The Violence Against Women Act Is a Failure

Respecting Accuracy in Domestic Abuse Reporting (R.A.D.A.R.)

Respecting Accuracy in Domestic Abuse Reporting (R.A.D.A.R.) argues in this viewpoint that the Violence Against Women Act (VAWA) is not working. VAWA-funded programs, says the author, often prohibit effective couples therapy. Services for female abusers or male victims in VAWA-funded programs often are non-existent, says R.A.D.A.R., though women initiate violence as often as men. R.A.D.A.R. argues that VAWA-funded services for male abusers are ineffective and restraining orders and mandatory arrest policies do not prevent domestic violence. R.A.D.A.R.—Respecting Accuracy in Domestic Abuse Reporting—is a non-profit, non-partisan organization of men and women working to improve the effectiveness of our nation's approach to solving domestic violence.

"U.S. Policy to Reduce Violence Against Women Creates Injustice Instead," by Respecting Accuracy in Domestic Abuse Reporting. Excerpted from Respecting Accuracy in Domestic Abuse Reporting, "Why Have Domestic Violence Programs Failed to Stop Partner Abuse?" RADAR website at www.mediaradar.org, 2007. For the complete and unabridged version of this report, including extensive supporting footnotes, see http://www.mediaradar.org/docs/RADARreport-Why-DV-Programs-Fail-to-Stop-Abuse.pdf.

As you read, consider the following questions:

1. What percentage of 30 states analyzed in a study referenced by the authors prohibit couples counseling?

2. According to psychologist Donald Dutton, quoted by the author, what effect does Duluth-related treatment have on domestic violence recidivism?

3. What are some of the reasons given for violation of restraining orders?

The enactment of the Violence Against Women Act in 1994 was a major milestone in our efforts to combat intimate partner assault. But more than a decade later, there is a growing recognition that our current approach to curbing intimate partner aggression is not working. Department of Justice officials openly acknowledge the problem:

- *"My perspective is someone who was a domestic-violence and sexual-assault prosecutor for 14 years, and I worked in a women's shelter one night a week. The experience for those people is that it [domestic violence] has not gone down."* —Cindy Dyer, Director, Office on Violence Against Women

- *"We have no evidence to date that VAWA has led to a decrease in the overall levels of violence against women."* —Angela Moore Parmley, PhD, Department of Justice

This Special Report analyzes the effectiveness of four key violence-reduction strategies currently employed by VAWA-funded programs:

1. Treatment Services

2. Restraining Orders

3. Mandatory Arrest

4. No-Drop Prosecution

1. Treatment Services

The dynamics of domestic violence are varied and complex. Partner aggression is influenced by factors such as marital status, age, socio-economic level, drug and alcohol use, psychological disorders, childhood abuse experiences, and conflict resolution skills.

Effective treatment should be based on a careful clinical assessment and tailored to the psychological and social needs of both the abuser and the partner. Above all, treatment services should be based on sound scientific research and the best practices of the counseling profession.

Couples Counseling

A key factor in the treatment of partner abuse is whether the physical aggression is mutual. Studies typically reveal that at least half of all abuse is reciprocal and is initiated by males and females at similar rates. For example, a recent CDC study found half of all partner violence was reciprocal. The 32-nation International Dating Violence Survey reported that 70% of all physical abuse was mutual. Logic dictates that counseling for both partners is essential for a successful resolution.

But under current domestic violence programs, couples counseling rarely happens. Why? Because many in the domestic violence industry adhere to an ideological belief that only men are capable of perpetrating domestic violence, and that women are only victims—a view wholly unsupported by scientific research.

As a result, treatment standards actually discourage family therapy. One analysis of 30 states implementing standards for offender treatment programs found that 42% of those states prohibit couples counseling.

These restrictions on couples therapy have become a point of contention between VAWA-funded batterer intervention providers and mental health providers. Couples therapy has been shown to be effective in treating violent partners. But by policy or by law, VAWA-funded programs often prohibit use of such services.

Services for Female Victims: Women's Shelters

The more than 1,200 abuse shelters in the United States are the mainstay of treatment services for female abuse victims. But what happens inside the protective walls of these shelters?

Feminist therapists advocate that women in shelters should be counseled to view their predicament as a consequence of patriarchy, despite a distinct lack of evidence to support that ideological stance. One national survey found that 45% of shelters viewed their main role as promoting feminist political activism, while only 25% focused on providing treatment and support for abused women.

An over-reliance on untrained volunteers is worrisome. One early report admitted, "It is the policy of many shelters to have the majority of their staffs comprised of such [abused] women because they can offer invaluable empathy to victims." One former shelter director noted, "The volunteers were sometimes more of a problem than they were worth because they were still dealing with their own personal issues."

Two anecdotal reports raise concerns about the services that shelters provide:

- A former participant in a support group found the real message of the group was to "accept the indoctrination and embrace my victimhood. . . . I realized that I never heard a facilitator encourage a woman to heal and move on with her life. They encouraged women to stay stuck in the victim mentality."

- A woman who attended group sessions later admitted that the group made her feel worse because "everyone was supposed to hate the men and want to leave them."

Although researchers have studied women's shelters for more than 20 years, the quality of the studies has been poor and the findings inconclusive. Such analyses typically lack pre-intervention data or comparison groups and fail to take into account critical variables.

Services for Female Abusers

Extensive research shows women are at least as likely as men to engage in partner aggression. Fewer than one in five cases of female violence are justified by the need for women to act in self-defense. Female-initiated violence is a cause for concern not only because of the physical and psychological effects on her partner, but also because it raises the concern of retaliatory aggression.

When abusive women request help from VAWA-funded agencies, they discover, much to their surprise, that requests for treatment are dismissed (often with a comment such as "He must have done something to provoke you") or that female-specific services are simply non-existent.

> *Darlene Hilker of Florida assaulted her husband. "I grabbed my husband's genitals—that's what I was arrested for," she later admitted. In 2006, the judge ordered her to attend the Women Who Batter program, one of the first such programs ever established in the United States.*

Services for Male Victims

The lack of services for male victims of domestic violence is well documented. One survey of 26 domestic violence shelters in California acknowledged, "Most shelters do not admit males." The former director of a shelter in the mid-Atlantic region revealed, "The shelter did not provide services to male victims of domestic violence, even when they had suffered physical abuse similar to that experienced by women."

In 2002, abuse victim Ray Blumhorst contacted 10 shelters in southern California to request help. All 10 shelters turned him down. When the shelters were later sued for discrimination, they chose to ignore the stated intent of Congress that "Men who have suffered these types of violent attacks are eligible ... for services and benefits that are funded under ... the Violence Against Women Act". The shelters believed that discrimination was their right, and went to court to defend that "right."

> *A college student who wishes to remain anonymous writes, "I am a male survivor and former victim of relationship abuse. I was mentally hijacked, emotionally destroyed, and physically beaten by my girlfriend for almost 3 years.... I remember being huddled on the floor ... as I watched, not felt, her beat me until she couldn't lift her arms anymore.... After a year of therapy, I still haven't found a support group for abused men."*

Services for Male Abusers

Male offenders are often ordered to attend a Batterer Intervention Program (BIP) as an alternative to incarceration. BIPs are typically based on the "Duluth Model" devised by the Duluth Domestic Abuse Intervention Project.

The Duluth approach does not resemble psychological counseling in the usual sense of the word. Duluth interventionists do not try to develop a therapeutic relationship with the clients, even though that relationship is the single most important predictor of psychological improvement. Duluth-adherents do not even make a clinical diagnosis because they believe it could provide a "rationalization for behavior that may not be accurate."

Rather, the Duluth Model is better viewed as a penal intervention that emphasizes monitoring and group shaming over treatment and rehabilitation. Psychologist James Kline believes these interventionists act as quasi-probation officers, noting that such individuals "have such narrow training and such indoctrination into the batterer model" of intimate-partner violence, that it leaves them "inadequate" as diagnosticians and counselors.

The decidedly ideological flavor of such efforts is revealed by a New York program whose website explains: "The Domestic Violence Program for Men provides important, serious analysis and topics that explore the roots of sexism, racism and the other oppressions which contribute to the systemic problems leading to much of the violence men commit against their intimate partners."

No surprise that such programs often have drop-out rates of over 80%. And no wonder the National Research Council deplored the fact that these programs are "driven by ideology and stakeholder interests rather than by plausible theories and scientific evidence of cause."

Psychologist Donald Dutton notes, "Research shows that Duluth-oriented treatments are absolutely ineffective, and have no discernible impact on rates of recidivism."

Even the sponsor of one such program says they don't work. The New York Model for Batterer Programs admits that "Decades of anecdotal reports from partners of men in programs and millions of dollars of research provide the answer: inconclusive, insignificant results."

Summary

This review of research and policy reveals an ironic pattern of available services that are *in*effective, along with a general unavailability of services that *are* effective:

- For partners engaged in mutual violence, couples counseling is usually discouraged and often prohibited.

- For female victims, no good evidence supports the effectiveness of abuse shelters.

- For female abusers, VAWA services are generally unavailable.

- For male victims, VAWA-funded programs are virtually non-existent.

- For male abusers, Duluth model treatment programs are flatly ineffective.

In her article on treatment of male abusers, "The evolution of battering interventions", psychologist Julia Babcock asks, "Is the Duluth model set up to fail?" In light of these research findings, one might conclude that the entire spectrum of VAWA-funded treatment programs has been set up for failure.

2. Restraining Orders

Restraining orders, sometimes known as "orders for protection," are commonly used to combat domestic violence. They are a legal directive ordering an individual to avoid contact and communication with his partner for a specified period of time.

2–3 million domestic restraining orders are issued each year in the United States. Only half of all restraining orders involve any allegation of physical violence—the reason being that states now define domestic "violence" so broadly that non-violent acts are included.

Restraining orders would seem to be an easy solution to a difficult problem, but experience suggests they are no solution.

One report stated flatly, "All observers agree that—at least until they are violated—a civil protection order is useless with the 'hard core' batterer ... Any abuser who is determined to batter—or kill—his [or her] partner will not be deterred by a piece of paper."

A study published in the *American Journal of Public Health* followed 150 women who met initial screening criteria for a permanent restraining order. 81 of the women received the requested order; 69 did not. Over the subsequent 18 months, the women who'd been granted the order reported the same levels of threats, physical abuse, and stalking as the women who were not granted an order.

Restraining orders are hardly the panacea that their advocates once envisioned. As the Independent Women's Forum has concluded, restraining orders seem to only "lull women into a false sense of security."

3. Mandatory Arrest

Mandatory Arrest for Assault

Mandatory arrest for partner assault has been hotly debated over the past 25 years. The 1981–1982 Minneapolis Domestic Violence Experiment suggested that arrest led to substantial reductions in subsequent violence, but that study's short follow-up period and small sample size calls the results into question.

Follow-up studies in Colorado Springs and Milwaukee came to the opposite conclusion, finding that mandatory arrest policies can cause an increase, rather than a decrease, in domestic violence.

Harvard economist Radha Iyengar analyzed the impact of the passage of mandatory arrest laws in 15 states. Her surprising conclusion: "Intimate partner homicides increased by about 60% in states with mandatory arrest laws," which means that, "Mandatory arrest laws are responsible for an additional 0.8 murders per 100,000 people."

Mandatory Arrest for Restraining Order Violations

33 states mandate arrest for violation of a restraining order. Yet breaches of such orders are common and occur for a variety of reasons. Although in some cases the offender continues to harass the victim, in other cases the couple decides to re-unite but forgets to have the order rescinded. And in some cases the claimant intentionally entraps the alleged abuser:

Rob was removed from his home and forbidden to have any contact with his son. After several months, Rob's wife told him she'd changed her mind and asked him to come pick up their son. Shortly after Rob reached the house, a Sheriff's Deputy arrived.

Unbeknownst to Rob, after asking him how long it would be until he arrived at his former home, his wife had called in a violation of the restraining order. Rob was arrested for the restraining order violation and their son was placed in temporary foster care.

There is no evidence that prosecution of restraining order violations reduces subsequent abuse, and one Department of Justice-funded study concluded, "Increases in the willingness of prosecutors' offices to take cases of protection order violation were associated with *increases in the homicide* of White married intimates, Black unmarried intimates, and White unmarried females."

Mandatory arrest policies may be an applause-grabbing sound-bite for politicians. But as a law enforcement tool, they have proven to be a failure.

4. No-Drop Prosecution

The majority of abuse cases involve disputes in which the conflict is a minor, mutual, and/or one-time occurrence. The victim often believes that these situations can be better handled through counseling or a brief "cooling-off" period rather than legal intervention. So, in about 80% of cases, the person who requests police assistance later recants or drops the charges.

But roughly 2/3 of prosecutors offices have instituted "no-drop" policies requiring them to ignore the claimant's request and prosecute the case regardless.

No-drop policies do a disservice to both alleged abusers and victims. By eliminating prosecutorial discretion they increase the likelihood of frivolous legal action. If the defendant is poor, he or she has to rely on the counsel of an already over-burdened public defender. In many cases, the accused is compelled to accept a plea bargain that requires admitting to having committed a lesser crime, even if no violence occurred.

When an alleged victim refuses to testify, prosecutors often charge obstruction of justice and threaten to take away the children. In one such case a woman who was jailed for refusing to testify against her boyfriend won a $125,000 settlement for false imprisonment. However in most cases, the woman succumbs to the coercion and says whatever the prosecutor wants, regardless of the truth or falsehood of her initial accusations.

Overly aggressive prosecution policies dissuade women from seeking future police assistance. One survey of female victims in Quincy, Massachusetts, found that among women who did not report a subsequent incident of abuse, 56% believed that the victim has no say or rights in the criminal justice system.

Only one randomized study has evaluated the effectiveness of varying levels of prosecution on subsequent aggression. The research found that only one factor reduced abuser recidivism—allowing the victim to select whether and how aggressively the prosecutor would pursue the case. No-drop prosecution eliminates the chance for the victim to make that choice.

A Department of Justice analysis reached this sobering conclusion: "We do not know whether no-drop increases victim safety or places the victims in greater jeopardy."

Symbols Over Substance

Declines in intimate partner homicides began in the mid-1970s, and trends continued on the same course following passage of VAWA in 1994. For non-fatal abuse of women, trends over the past decade were similar regardless of whether the perpetrator was a friend, stranger, or intimate. Hence, there is no evidence that the Violence Against Women Act has reduced partner violence.

Scores of scientific studies reveal:

- Abuser treatment services are either ineffective, or those known to be effective are generally unavailable.

- Restraining orders generally have no impact on subsequent physical abuse.

- Mandatory arrest laws substantially increase homicides, discourage future requests for police assistance, and reduce conviction rates.

- We do not know whether no-drop prosecution increases, reduces, or has no impact on future violence.

Thus, VAWA-funded programs appear to be ineffective and sometimes harmful. Whether viewed at the level of aggregate crime statistics or specific abuse reduction strategies, our nation's approach to curbing partner violence has been a failure.

Others have reached a similar conclusion:

- Noted family violence researcher Richard Gelles stated, "Policy and practice based on these factoids and theory might actually be harmful to women, men, children, and the institution of the family."

- New York University vice provost Linda Mills concluded: "At worst, the criminal justice system increases violence against women. At best, it has little or no effect."

So why have ineffective, and possibly harmful, policies been allowed to persist?

University of Hawaii law professor Virginia Hench notes that these policies are "a classic example of a 'get tough' policy that has symbolic value with the electorate, but which can lead to a host of problems." Hench concludes that if we "choose symbols over substance, that is a true failure to support those victims" of violence.

It is time that we implemented effective solutions to partner abuse—solutions based not on ideology or the symbols of political posturing, but rather on the sound foundation of valid science and well-tested professional practice.

"*[Mandatory] arrest can indeed be protective against domestic violence escalating to lethality.*"

Mandatory Arrest Policies Help Prevent Domestic Violence

Rasmieyh Abdelnabi

In the following viewpoint, Rasmieyh Abdelnabi argues that the police support mandatory arrests of domestic violence perpetrators because arresting such persons can prevent injuries to their victims or intended victims as well as facilitate getting help for the abuser. Prompt arrests can prevent domestic violence from escalating, the author contends, adding that arrests also teach children that domestic violence is wrong and may prevent them from committing similar acts when they become adults. Rasmieyh Abdelnabi writes for the Beloit Daily News *in Beloit, Wisconsin.*

As you read, consider the following questions:

1. According to the author, why are those arrested for domestic violence not incarcerated for very long?

Rasmieyh Abdelnabi, "Domestic Violence Law Not Causing Inmate Increase," *Beloit (WI) Daily News*, January 4, 2007. Reproduced by permission.

2. According to law enforcement statistics quoted by Abdelnabi, what happens when police responding to a domestic violence call only warn rather than arrest?

3. Based on law enforcement surveys cited by the author, how do most law enforcement agencies feel about the mandatory arrest law?

The Mandatory Arrest Law concerning domestic violence recently was discussed as a possible reason Rock County [Wisconsin] Jail's inmate population is growing.

However, experts said this is unlikely and there are supporters of the law.

During a recent [meeting of the] Rock County Criminal Justice Coordinating Council, members raised concerns over reasons for jailing people. Some claimed too many people were being arrested on domestic abuse–related offenses because of a law requiring mandatory arrest.

Intervention, Not Jail, the Goal

Lt. Bill Harper of Rock County Sheriff's Department said domestic abuse–related arrests are not necessarily the reason for an increase in the jail population.

"In the short term, yes, we have to book them and they might have to stay overnight to go to court. But [while] I don't think it has a huge impact on jail housing, it does have some," he explained.

He explained while people are jailed for domestic abuse–related offenses, they usually post bond very quickly as the bond amount is not very high.

"The system intervenes so there is a quicker opportunity to order them into counseling to try to address the problem and not necessarily just the symptoms," Harper said.

Preventing Escalation

There seems to be a lot of support for the Mandatory Arrest Law because it could prevent someone from getting injured, he said.

Beloit Police Capt. Bill Tyler said mandatory arrest allows for a cooling off period.

Law enforcement agents have discretion when it comes to arresting someone on domestic violence charges since charges encompass many issues, ranging from actual physical harm to threats and criminal damage to property, he said.

"Typically the officer needs to identify the primary aggressor," Tyler explained. "The push is to be able to make an arrest whenever possible if you can make out the circumstances."

Before the law was implemented officers would respond to the same domestic situation three or four times a night.

"Just because they tell people to knock it off doesn't mean that's going to happen," said Executive Director Patti Seger of the Wisconsin Coalition Against Domestic Violence. "Every time they went back, the violence was escalating, it was getting worse and worse. Not only was it getting dangerous for the family, it was also getting dangerous for (officers). This has been a great tool for them to take people of out the situation."

Arrest, Not Incarceration, Is Mandatory

Seger said the law is really not about incarcerating people, it's about helping them.

"It's not a mandatory incarceration law. (Victims) want the violence to end but they don't necessarily want their abusers to end up in prison. What they want is for someone to intervene and stop the violence," she explained.

Victims Should Not Be Arrested

Domestic violence cases are typically misdemeanors, unless serious or fatal injuries occurred. Those arrested on other mis-

Pro-Arrest Policies Necessary

Pro-arrest policies are seen by many as necessary to combat a long-standing and globally prevalent police attitude that domestic violence is not a crime. Research also indicates that arrests may deter future lethal violence. A 2003 study, described in the *American Journal of Public Health* and reported in a release by the Family Violence Prevention Fund, found that a batterer's prior arrest for domestic violence "actually decreased the risk for femicide" and concluded that "arrest can indeed be protective against domestic violence escalating to lethality."

Stop Violence Against Women,
February 1, 2006. www.stopvaw.org.

demeanor charges sometimes spend a night in jail, so why not apply the same standards to domestic abuse charges, Seger said.

In recent years, she said less have been arrested on domestic abuse charges. However, more victims are seeking services and this could be for a number of reasons. One reason is that victims are electing not to go to police, Seger said.

The Mandatory Arrest Law was passed in 1988 and implemented in April 1989. Some amendments have been made to better explain what is required of law enforcement agencies and to tighten language.

Soon after its implementation, victims were arrested along with their aggressors because they may have fought back to protect themselves, Seger explained.

In 1990, an amendment to the law was made to prevent victims from being arrested.

"However, over the last few years, we saw a spike in victims being arrested," Seger said.

In 2006, additional amendments were made to prevent victims from being arrested and to put more focus on arresting the primary physical aggressor, she said.

"It's too new a law, too new a change to really see if law enforcement is not arresting victims because obviously the information is not available to us yet," Seger explained.

Teaching Children

As the law has changed over the last several years, so has society's attitude toward domestic violence, she said.

"For many years law enforcement used to see domestic violence as a private matter, it was a social matter," Seger said. "If a stranger hit another person it was considered a crime. Domestic violence was not considered a crime. Now most law enforcement agencies support the mandatory arrest law. Many of them see the inter-generational component to domestic violence. Many talk about seeing that play out in their career and seeing how domestic violence is connected to other crimes."

Children who see the abuse in their homes may grow up and commit similar acts, continuing the cycle of violence.

"Police now are seeing it as an opportunity, in a timely way to confer to young children that the violence that happens in the home is a criminal act," Seger said.

"The certainty of arrest dissuades victims from reporting abuse to the police resulting in higher rates of intimate partner abuse."

Mandatory Arrests Increase Domestic Violence

Radha Iyengar

In the following viewpoint, Radha Iyengar argues that mandatory arrest policies actually increase domestic violence because the policy discourages reporting of abuse by victims. Analysis of data, she contends, shows that an increase in intimate homicides has occurred in states with mandatory arrest policies. According to Iyengar, mandatory arrest policies were adopted in response to lawsuit liability for domestic violence and were promoted based on research that failed to take into account the effect that the policies would have on the reporting of domestic violence. Mandatory arrests, the author concludes, deters victims' reporting rather than perpetrators' abuse. Radha Iyengar is Robert Wood Johnson Scholar in Health Policy Research at Harvard University.

As you read, consider the following questions:

1. According to the author, during the 1970s, what did the American Bar Association urge police to use, instead of making arrests, when dealing with domestic violence?
2. What domestic violence experiment does Iyengar say was used to justify mandatory arrest policies?
3. According to the author, what has been the impact of mandatory arrest policies on the number of intimate partner homicides in the United States?

Women are more likely to be beaten, raped, or killed by a current or former male partner than by anyone else. Despite two decades of increased public awareness, domestic violence remains a serious public policy issue in the United States. States, faced with increased liability for police inaction in the mid-eighties to late-nineties, passed laws requiring the warrantless arrests of individuals police believe to be responsible for misdemeanor assault of an intimate partner. Many of these policies were justified by results from a randomized experiment that demonstrated that arrests were effective at deterring future violence. This experiment was extended to support mandating arrest in all cases of domestic violence. However, the experiment provided no evidence on the effectiveness of a public policy *requiring* arrest. Policies which mandate arrest (i.e. make arrests certain, conditional on reporting) may have a different result from experiments which probabilistically apply arrest. Indeed the empirical analysis presented [here] demonstrates that mandatory arrest laws increase intimate partner homicides. One reason for this is that a known policy of arrest may affect the decision by victims to seek police intervention making the application of experimental results to the public policy of required arrests inappropriate. In particular, it appears that the certainty of arrest dissuades victims from reporting abuse to the police resulting in higher rates of intimate partner abuse.

Policy Increases Homicides

Using a difference-in-difference framework, I tested to see if mandatory arrest laws affected the level of domestic violence. I found that intimate partner homicides increased by about 60 percent in states with mandatory arrest laws. These results may be due to changes in the reporting behavior of victims in response to the certainty of arrest. Because police intervention may decrease the risk of escalation and thus the risk of homicides, this rise in homicide rates is consistent with a decline in reporting for intimate partner homicides. Results from a similar analysis of non-intimate partner family member homicides show declines in these homicides in response to mandatory arrest laws. These results are also consistent with the reporting explanation. In most cases of child abuse, the reporting of abuse comes from a third party (such as a teacher or doctor). In such cases the certainty of arrest does not shift the incentives of the third party to report, and as such we would expect to see a deterrence effect from arrest. Thus, the declines in familial homicides represent evidence consistent with the theory that a decline in reporting by victims may be responsible for the perverse effects of mandatory arrest laws.

This study attempts to provide a careful evaluation of a public policy that currently enjoys both popular and financial support. This enhanced understanding of the full range effects generated by arrest laws for domestic abuse will hopefully be useful in constructing a more effective criminal justice response to domestic violence. This paper also highlights an important consideration for policy makers; criminal justice policies aimed at deterring violence must concern themselves with both the probability of detection and the actual penalty enhancement. Laws like mandatory arrest laws may fail if the responsiveness of victims to incentives generated by these policies is larger than the response of criminals to the cost of the new penalty. Thus, increasing criminal sanctions without concern for the impact on the probability of detection may generate perverse outcomes from public policy. In addition, because of the powerful role the empirical social science research played in the case of this policy, this study provides a cautionary tale about using experimental results to justify new policies. The misapplication of experiments without concern for the ways in which policies might deviate from experiments may result in government programs that become counterproductive, harming the very people they seek to help.

Criminalization of Domestic Violence

Policies that encourage or require arrest of domestic abusers play a prominent role in the government's attempt to combat domestic violence. This is in part because the criminalization of domestic violence represented the major shift in the acceptance and treatment of domestic violence and in part because arrest laws represent a transparent mechanism by which the government can enforce anti-violence statutes.

The criminal justice response to intimate partner violence has been codified in many jurisdictions through policies which encourage or mandate the arrest of individuals who commit domestic abuse. Currently, fourteen states and the District of Columbia have passed mandatory arrest laws. These laws require police to arrest a suspect without a warrant, if there is probable cause to suspect that an individual has committed some form of assault (either misdemeanor or felonious) against an intimate partner or family member. An additional eight states have recommended arrest laws, which specify arrest as recommended but not required when confronted with probable cause that an intimate partner or familial assault has occurred. . . .

To begin an evaluation of arrest laws for domestic abuse, it is first necessary to establish why these laws were initially passed. Mandatory arrest laws appear to have been passed largely in response to a court decision in Connecticut as well as what many took to be empirical support for arrest from a randomized experiment. Nevertheless, we might be skeptical of any subsequent analysis attempting to establish the causal effect of arrest laws on domestic violence if these laws were passed in response to a rising trend in domestic violence levels. This does not appear to be the case.

Historically, law enforcement has been reluctant to arrest or even intervene in cases of domestic violence. In fact in the 1970s, the American Bar Association (1973) urged police to use conflict resolution, not arrests, when intervening in "conflicts ... which occur between husband and wife." In the early eighties this began to change as attitudes towards domestic violence changed. Increasingly, there was political pressure for states to offer more protection for victims of domestic violence. Moreover, there was a shift in the medical opinion regarding the dangers posed to victims of domestic violence. For instance, the American Medical Association began to advise its members that counseling was dangerous and increased its [efforts] to educate its members about the harms of domestic violence.

Lawsuits and the Minnesota Experiment

The emergence of mandatory arrest laws occurred within this environment, largely prompted by two events. First, *Thurman v. City of Torrington* (1984), a law suit in Connecticut, established the right to police protection from domestic violence. Threats of future law suits served as motivation for municipalities to protect themselves from liability issues by implementing more aggressive arrest policies. The establishment of police liability in domestic violence cases created the desire to monitor and regulate police enforcement of restraining orders and intervention in violent incidents. A natural means to do this was the removal of police discretion through a policy which mandated arrest. However, arrest policies might not have been so widely adopted had it not been for the second event—the Minnesota Domestic Violence Experiment. The results of this experiment were used by US Department of Justice, academics, legislators, and criminal justice spokespersons to justify and support mandatory arrest policies. For example, the Violence Against Women Act (1994) used the results from this experiment to justify grants and funds to support pro-arrest policies in various states. This change in funding and availability of training encouraged several more states to pass mandatory arrest laws

The use of mandatory arrest laws was thus in many respects predicated on the results of the Minnesota Domestic Violence Experiment (MDVE). This experiment, funded by the Minnesota Police Department, the Police Foundation, and the Department of Justice, was run by randomly assigning a police response to domestic violence calls. Police applied one of three possible treatments: (1) advising and counseling the couple, (2) separating the individuals, or (3) arresting the suspect. Researchers then interviewed the victims shortly after police involvement and then followed up every two weeks for six months. The original results found that arresting the suspect resulted in substantially less future violence than did either advising or counseling. An in depth evaluation of the results by [Helen] Tauchen and [Ann Dryden] Witte found that arrest resulted in significantly more deterrence than either advising or separating the couple, consistent with the original findings of the experiment. However, unlike the original findings, Tauchen and Witte used a dynamic setting which found that most of the deterrent effect of arrest occurs within two weeks of the initial arrest. Thus, any deterrent effect that exists is highly transitory.

While this experiment provided support for the contention that arrest deters abuse, the applicability of the findings is uncertain. The public in general and battered women in particular were not informed of this experiment. Thus, the experiment actually tested the effect of a probabilistic arrest rather than a deterministic policy which requires arrest. This

Mandatory Arrest Policies Are Flawed

Despite the lack of empirical evidence for the efficacy of mandatory policies, they are in place in 24 states. And all 50 states have some form of de facto mandatory (preferred or pro-arrest) domestic violence policies. The obvious problems created by placing the *dangerous cart* (mandatory policies) before the *protective horse* (a coordinated community response) continues to be ignored by advocates and public policy makers.

Richard Davis, "Mandatory Arrest: A Flawed Policy Based on a False Premise," March 31, 2008. www.policeone.com.

difference is significant because of behavioral differences that may arise in an ongoing nature of the relationship between the battered women and their abusers. A noteworthy difference between a mandatory arrest policy and the MDVE is the potential response by battered women to the certainty of an arrest of their abuser. The response by batterers relative to the response by victims to the increased costs of abuse may be relevant when determining the efficacy of an intervention such as mandatory arrest laws.

Thus, while a full discussion of the political economy of the emergence of domestic violence laws is beyond the scope of this paper, the motivation of most of these arrest laws does not appear to have been the level of intimate partner violence. In a detailed analysis of the motivations for mandatory arrest laws, [E.] Stark states that the most important reason for passing mandatory arrest laws was controlling police behavior in response to political pressure and liability exposure. Reducing the level of violence was actually only of distant concern after the desire to stop immediate violence and avoid liability from inaction. Additionally, in as much as public pressure existed regarding the passage of these laws, this pressure was not due to the level of violence but rather perceived government treatment of offenders. For example, [Eve] Buzawa and [Carl] Buzawa argue that alternative reforms (such as mediation) were dismissed as inappropriate or sexist as American society became more conservative and punitive towards offenders. Thus, while these laws were not passed as parts of omnibus "tough on crime" legislation, they represent the desire to adopt a more punitive approach to crime. . . .

Mandatory Arrests Increase Homicides

To test the effectiveness of mandatory arrest laws, I consider the effect of these laws on intimate partner abuse. This requires special attention to the total number of incidents of domestic violence not simply the number of reported incidents because the fraction of incidents that are reported to the police is potentially affected by this policy. If I cannot observe unreported incidents, changes in the number of reported incidents and change in the total number of incidents (both reported and unreported) are observationally equivalent. In part because I can observe victim-offender relationship and in part because these crimes are almost perfectly reported, I use measure of intimate partner homicides as a way to measure intimate partner abuse. Assuming that police intervention can reduce the probability of violence, changes in the intimate partner homicide measure may provide insight into the impact of mandatory arrest laws on intimate partner violence. . . .

To construct a dataset of intimate partner homicides, I use the FBI Uniform Crime Reports, Supplementary Homicide Reports that provide data for all homicides that took place in the years 1976 to 2003 in all 50 states and the District of Columbia, with additional descriptive variables about the victim, offender, and the nature of the crime. I define an intimate partner homicide to include any homicide committed against a husband, wife, common-law husband, common-law wife, ex-husband, or ex-wife. . . .

The results suggest that mandatory arrest laws are responsible for an additional 0.8 murders per 100,000 people. This corresponds to a 54 percent increase in intimate partner homicides. . . .

Why Reduced Reporting?

In the case of domestic violence, victims may bear the costs of an increased penalty to the abusers in several ways: First, there is a psychological and emotional component of intimate partner abuse that often generates victims who remain committed to their abuser and do not wish to send him to prison. Thus, guilt effectively transfers the cost from abusers to victims. Second, if abusers are arrested but no further legal action is taken, they may return home within a day of their arrest and further terrorize their victim. In a non-experimental evaluation of mandatory arrest as a policy, [Andrea] Lyon used a logistic model to compare the likelihood of arrest under mandatory arrest laws versus pro-arrest laws in two cities in Michigan. She found that once a victim calls the police to report an incident, she is significantly less likely to call again. She posits this was likely because police intervention in the form of an arrest resulted in retribution by the abuser, deterring future reporting. Third, in many cases, arrests laws resulted in the victim also being arrested if there was evidence that she (or he) physically assaulted her (or his) partner. In many areas, women constitute nearly 20 percent of domestic violence arrests, a far higher percentage than the estimated proportion of female abusers. Over half of these female arrestees can be identified as previous victims of intimate partner violence. Anecdotal evidence from some battered women advocates suggests that these "dual arrests" are the most serious problem with mandatory arrest. Dual arrests have serious implications for victims who are immigrants and may be deported if convicted of assault. In addition, those who have children face potential loss of custody during the arrest period. All of these costs may result in an increased unwillingness to report abuse to the police. . . .

Many states use laws requiring the warrantless arrest of individuals believed to be responsible for intimate partner abuse as a major policy tool in their effort to end domestic violence. The results presented in this study suggest that this may in fact be counterproductive. Using data from the FBI Supplementary Homicide Reports from 1976–2003, I find that the level of intimate partner homicide increased in states with these mandatory arrest laws. This may be because abuse victims may be less likely to contact the police in the face of a mandatory arrest law. This failure to contact the police results in fewer interventions risking an increased probability of escalating violence. . . .

The irony that a mandatory arrest law intended to deter abuse actually increases intimate partner homicides is not lost on this author. Given the dangerous and pervasive nature of domestic violence, there is little doubt that state intervention, in some form, is required. Determining what shape that intervention takes is of vital importance. The results from this study suggest that the threat of arrest is insufficient to deter abusers from killing their victims. Finding arrests deter victim reporting rather than perpetrator abuse provides valuable insight into the intricacies facing governmental attempts to decrease intimate partner violence. While it appears that mandatory arrest laws are not sufficient to deter abuse, the set of policies that can effectively prevent abuse and protect victims remains an issue for future research

> *"Male offenders were more than twice as likely as women charged with similar crimes to be incarcerated for more than a year, and . . . women were more likely to receive a light sentence."*

Women Receive Disproportionately Lighter Sentences than Men in Domestic Violence Cases

Cathy Young

In the following viewpoint, Cathy Young argues that the legal system and society in general discriminate against men accused of domestic violence. She cites specific examples of cases in which women who pleaded guilty to domestic violence charges were given disproportionately light sentences when compared with men who faced similar charges. While most feminists and women's rights advocates tend to excuse the legal system's leniency toward women, arguing that most of the time the accused have been provoked to violence, some say that excusing women's violence on the grounds of emotional problems may un-

Cathy Young, "License to Kill: Men and Women, Crime and Punishment (Disproportionately Light Sentences Given to Women)," *Reason*, vol. 24, July 2002, pp. 22–23. Copyright © 2002 by Reason Foundation, 3415 S. Sepulveda Blvd., Suite 400, Los Angeles, CA 90034, www.reason.com. Reproduced by permission.

dercut women's ability to been seen as capable workers and lead-
ers in the long run. *Cathy Young writes a column for the* Boston
Globe *and is the author of* Cease-fire! Why Women and Men
Must Join Forces to Achieve True Equality.

As you read, consider the following questions:

1. What was the full sentence for Brenda Working's attempted murder of her husband, as reported by Young?
2. What percentage of women who pleaded guilty to killing their spouses received prison sentences, according to
   a 1988 Justice Department study cited by the author?
3. Why do anti–domestic violence advocates claim that
   women kill, according to Young?

Late one night in August 1997, a Tacoma, Washington,
woman named Brenda Lee Working called her estranged
husband, Michael, and told him that her car had broken down,
stranding her and their two preschool daughters in a wooded
area on a military base. When Michael Working came to her
aid, it turned out to be an ambush. Brenda shot him several
times, hitting him in the arm and the shoulder. Then she beat
him in the face with the handgun as he tried to wrench it
from her hands and stalked him through the woods for hours
after he managed to get away.

Brenda Working's sentence for the attempted murder of
her husband: one day in jail.

Admittedly, this was not the full extent of Working's punishment: She received a separate five-year sentence for using a
gun in the commission of a crime. Yet the sentencing judge,
U.S. District Judge Jack Tanner, openly stated that he would
have suspended that sentence too if it had not been mandatory under federal law. His reasoning was that Working had
been depressed and fearful that her estranged husband would
take away her children in a custody battle. . . .

The U.S. Court of Appeals for the 9th Circuit overturned
the sentence, ruling that Tanner had improperly departed

from the sentencing guidelines without adequate reasons. The case was sent back to the lower court and reassigned to another judge. The 9th Circuit's ruling made an unusual explicit reference to gender bias, stating that Tanner "would be unlikely to set aside considerations of Working's sex."

Gender-Based Leniency Toward Women

Despite the eventual outcome, many would say the Working case illustrates a pervasive pattern in the criminal justice system of gender-based leniency toward women. This has become an article of faith among men's rights activists. In his 1993 book *The Myth of Male Power*, Warren Farrell asserts that "twelve distinct female-only defenses allow a woman who commits a premeditated murder to have the charges dropped or significantly reduced."

This sensational claim is seriously exaggerated. Of the 12 items listed by Farrell, only three—insanity pleas based on premenstrual syndrome or postpartum depression and self-defense or insanity pleas based on battered woman syndrome—can accurately be called "female-only defenses." (And even these defenses rarely succeed.)

The rest of Farrell's list consists of factors that contribute to more-lenient treatment of women, from stereotypes that make women less likely suspects to protective husbands standing by wives who have committed violence against them or their children.

Nonetheless, the pattern does exist. Two Justice Department studies in the late 1980s found that male offenders were more than twice as likely as women charged with similar crimes to be incarcerated for more than a year, and that even allowing for other factors, such as prior convictions, women were more likely to receive a light sentence.

Disparities in Family Murders

The disparities are especially striking in family murders, the primary form of homicide committed by women. A Justice

System Encourages False Accusations

[An American Bar Association] document called "Tool for Attorneys" provides lawyers with a list of suggestive questions to encourage their clients to make domestic-violence charges. Knowing that a woman can get a restraining order against the father of her children in an ex parte proceeding without any evidence, and that she will never be punished for lying, domestic-violence accusations have become a major tactic for securing sole child custody.

Phyllis Schlafly, May 17, 2006.
www.eagleforum.org.

Department study of domestic homicides in 1988 found that 94 percent of men who were convicted of (or pled guilty to) killing their spouses received prison sentences, but only 81 percent of the women did. The average sentence was 16.5 years for husbands and a mere six years for wives.

Some of the difference was due to the fact that more of the women had been "provoked"—that is, assaulted or threatened prior to the killing. But when there had been no provocation, the average prison sentence was seven years for killer wives and 17 years for killer husbands.

Beyond the numbers, the contrast between the treatment of male and female defendants can be shocking in individual cases.

In 1995, Texas executed Jesse Dewayne Jacobs for a murder that, by the prosecutors' admission, was committed by his sister, Bobbie Jean Hogan. Hogan—who had gotten Jacobs to help her abduct her boyfriend's ex-wife and had actually pulled the trigger—served 10 years in prison.

She was convicted only of involuntary manslaughter after her lawyers managed to persuade the jury that the gun went off accidentally.

Old-Fashioned Chivalry

Old-fashioned chivalry undoubtedly plays a role. "Women and men do occupy separate places in the collective psyche of society," Jonathan Last wrote approvingly in *The Weekly Standard* in 1998, shortly after the execution of ax murderer Karla Faye Tucker. "Because society has a low tolerance for seeing them harmed, women—even criminals—have traditionally been treated differently by the justice system. Differently, but still, at least possibly, with justice."

In recent years, this chivalry has declined. Yet while it is no longer acceptable to argue that female criminals are due special consideration because they're women, many feminists' insistence on seeing women as victims of patriarchy sometimes has the same effect.

Most anti–domestic violence activists, for instance, cling to the dogma that women kill only in response to male violence. The battered women's clemency movement has obtained pardons for female murderers who, as subsequent investigations found, had very flimsy claims of abuse and probably had been driven by "masculine" motives, such as jealousy.

Other cases never go to trial. In Brooklyn in 1987, Marlene Wagshall shot her sleeping husband, Joshua, in the stomach, crippling him for life, after finding a photo of him with a scantily clad woman. Wagshall was charged with attempted murder, but on the basis of her uncorroborated assertion that her husband had beaten her, District Attorney Elizabeth Holtzman, a strong champion of women's rights, let her plead guilty to assault with a sentence of one day in jail and five years' probation.

Feminist Response

Even when feminists do not actively defend violent women, they hardly ever speak up against inappropriate leniency toward female defendants. Mostly, they refuse to admit that such leniency exists—perhaps because it would be heresy to concede that "patriarchy" has sometimes worked in women's favor—and prefer to focus on real or mythical instances in which the justice system treats women more harshly. (Battered women's advocates have promoted the wholly fictional factoid that a woman who kills her mate is sentenced to an average of 15 to 20 years in prison, while a man gets two to six years.)

As a result, if a man commits a violent crime against a woman and gets off lightly, an outcry from women's groups often follows. If it's the other way round, the only vocal protests are likely to come from the victim's family and from prosecutors.

The Working case, like the Wagshall case, received minimal publicity. Imagine the reaction if a judge had said publicly that a man who had ambushed and shot his estranged wife should have been spared prison because he was depressed over the divorce.

There are feminists, such as Patricia Pearson, author of the 1997 book *When She Was Bad: Violent Women and the Myth of Innocence*, who find feminist paternalism toward women no less distasteful than the traditional kind. They argue that in the long run, excusing women's violence on the grounds of emotional problems may undercut women's ability to be seen as capable workers and leaders.

That may or may not happen. But even if women stand to lose nothing from the new double standards, any self-respecting feminist should still oppose them in the name of equal justice.

> *"Family court, ... perversely, concludes that women's attempts to protect their children [by leaving abusive men] actually demonstrate their own lack of fitness as mothers."*

The Legal System Fails to Protect Women Victimized by Domestic Violence

Harvard School of Public Health

In the following viewpoint, Harvard School of Public Health argues that family courts violate the human rights of women and their children. Although domestic violence is a recognized problem, courts give custody to abusive men, disregard evidence of domestic violence when determining custody, and fail to investigate documented child abuse, according to the author. These failures violate United Nations treaties and conventions. Harvard School of Public Health is dedicated to advancing public health through training, research, and communication.

Harvard School of Public Health, "Researchers Say Massachusetts Family Courts Fail to Protect Battered Women and Their Children: Study Applies Human Rights Analysis to Child Custody Cases Involving Domestic Violence," AScribe Law News Service, May 27, 2004. Copyright © 2004 AScribe. Reproduced by permission.

As you read, consider the following questions:

1. Family courts in what state were the subject of the study cited by the author as evidence of human rights violations?
2. According to the author, how do family courts view the threat to children posed by men who perpetrate domestic violence?
3. In the view of the author, state family courts fail to sufficiently consider the "right to due diligence" as described in what United Nations declaration concerning domestic violence?

Taking a novel approach to the analysis of child custody awards in cases where domestic violence is involved, researchers at Harvard School of Public Health (HSPH) have documented what they argue is a recurring pattern of potential human rights violations by the state and a failure to protect battered women and their children.

Examining litigation in Massachusetts family courts involving a sample of battered women, the researchers found that the courts consistently dismissed or minimized the relevance of the male partners' abuse in awarding custody of children to such men.

Violating United Nations Conventions

The researchers cited numerous human rights treaties and conventions meant to protect women and children from violence, including the UN Convention on the Rights of the Child and the UN Declaration on the Elimination of Violence Against Women. They argue that a human rights framework is an important tool for pressing the need for legal, social and political reform to address domestic violence and to protect women and children, the most common victims of such violence.

Domestic Violence Is Torture of Women

Domestic violence is a violation of a woman's rights to physical integrity, liberty, and all too often, her right to life itself. And when a government fails to provide effective protection from such abuse, domestic violence is torture.

Amnesty International,
"A Fact Sheet on Domestic Violence as Torture," 2007.
www.amnestyusa.org.

The analysis was performed by Jay Silverman, PhD, assistant professor of Society, Human Development and Health at HSPH, and colleagues and appears in the June issue of the *American Journal of Public Health*. Silverman is co-author of the book, *The Batterer as Parent*.

Major Public Health Concerns

Intimate partner violence and child abuse are increasingly recognized as major public health concerns in both the United States and around the world. According to the U.S. Department of Justice, one fourth of women in the United States are reported to be affected by intimate partner violence. In U.S. studies, male partners have been found responsible for one third of all homicides of women and half of all homicides of children.

Although there is increasing recognition of the great threat to children posed by men who perpetrate domestic violence, many family courts view such concerns as either irrelevant or a tactic to be ignored in cases of divorce, said Silverman. This failure directly leads to courts placing children in harm's way.

The researchers interviewed 39 women representing 10 of the 12 Massachusetts family court districts. The women were participants in the Battered Mothers' Testimony Project which drew women through social service agencies and legal providers serving battered women. The women all had experienced violence from an intimate male partner with whom they'd had children and had engaged in child custody litigation with the abusive ex-partner. As this study was an attempt to document human rights violations based on historic concerns regarding these processes from battered women and family violence experts throughout the country, women were also selected based on expressed dissatisfaction with the family court process. All possessed some kind of documentation of domestic violence (e.g. police reports, witness affidavits, restraining orders, child protective service reports). None of the cases involved women's abuse of male partners nor were there cases involving substantiated child abuse by the mothers.

Potential Human Rights Violations

Several themes emerged that corresponded to a consistent pattern of potential human rights violations by the Massachusetts family courts. According to the researchers, these included:

1. granting physical custody of children to men who had used violence against the mothers or both the mothers and their children

2. granting unsupervised visitation of children to men who had used such violence

3. failing to accept or consider documentation of domestic violence as relevant evidence in child custody determinations

4. failure to investigate allegations or consider documentation of child abuse

In light of international human rights declarations and treaties, wrote the researchers, the state family courts likely failed to sufficiently consider the "right to due diligence" as described in the UN Declaration on the Elimination of Violence Against Women; the "best interests of the child" as described in the Convention on the Rights of the Child; the right to "bodily integrity," a fundamental human right enshrined in both the Universal Declaration of Human Rights and the International Covenant on Civil and Political Rights; and the "right to equal protection" under the law described in the Universal Declaration of Human Rights.

A Perilous Irony

"Battered mothers face a perilous irony," said Silverman. "Authorities push these women to leave abusive men in order to protect their children. But women who can make this break then face family court, another authority, that often ignores this history of abuse as a threat to children's safety and, perversely, concludes that women's attempts to protect their children from these men actually demonstrate their own lack of fitness as mothers."

"Although our laws increasingly urge courts to make domestic violence a primary consideration in deciding child custody, implementation of these laws is inconsistent at best, and will likely remain so, without strong oversight," said Silverman. "Placing a human rights framework on child custody decisions involving domestic violence clarifies the critical need to reform the system in order to protect the rights and lives of battered women and their children."

"This is an issue everywhere in the country," he added, "and this same project is being conducted in several other states. This report is but one of many continuing attempts by organizations nationwide to make the voices of these women and their children heard."

Periodical Bibliography

The following articles have been selected to supplement the diverse views in this chapter:

Leila Abolfazli — "Violence Against Women Act (VAWA)," *Georgetown Journal of Gender & the Law*, 2006 Annual Review.

Rupaleem Bhuyan — "The Production of the 'Battered Immigrant' in Public Policy and Domestic Violence Advocacy," *Journal of Interpersonal Violence*, February 2008.

John Conyers Jr. — "The 2005 Reauthorization of the Violence Against Women Act," *Violence Against Women*, May 2007.

Victoria Frye, May Haviland, and Valli Rajah — "Dual Arrest and Other Unintended Consequences of Mandatory Arrest in New York City: A Brief Report," *Journal of Family Violence*, August 2007.

Georgetown Journal of Gender & the Law — "Federal Domestic Violence Law," vol. 8, no. 2, 2007.

Julie Goldenson, Robert Geffner, Sharon L. Foster, and Clark R. Clipson — "Female Domestic Violence Offenders: Their Attachment Security, Trauma Symptoms, and Personality Organization," *Violence and Victims*, January 1, 2007.

Keith Guzik — "The Agencies of Abuse: Intimate Abusers' Experience of Presumptive Arrest and Prosecution," *Law & Society Review*, March 2008.

Mindie Lazarus-Black and Patricia L. McCall — "The Politics of Place: Practice, Process, and Kinship in Domestic Violence Courts," *Human Organization*, July 1, 2006.

Monica Perez Trujillo and Stuart Ross — "Police Response to Domestic Violence," *Journal of Interpersonal Violence*, April 2008.

OPPOSING
VIEWPOINTS®
SERIES

CHAPTER 4

How Can Domestic Violence Be Prevented?

Chapter Preface

Christopher Kilmartin, a professor of psychology, has written that "[w]hen we see gender-based violence, women-hating is just around the corner. Therefore, if we can turn this attitude around, we can go a long way toward solving the problem." One way to change the attitude of a perpetrator of domestic violence is by using a batterer intervention program (BIP).

Many batterer intervention programs are based on the so-called Duluth model. The underlying rationale for BIPs stems from feminist theory, which asserts that patriarchal systems and culture encourage men to control their partners and condone men's violent behavior. The Duluth model requires men to confront their attitudes about control and teaches them other strategies for dealing with their partners. This model is the most common form of BIP in use today. However, critics contend that this approach utilizes "shame and blame" rather than therapy and can be applied only to male perpetrators, and is thus limited by the very principles of its theory. According to a review of BIP studies published by the National Institute for Justice, "Recent studies produce strong evidence that the Duluth model of batterer intervention is largely ineffective."

But are alternatives more effective than the Duluth model? Cognitive-behavioral interventions view battering as a result of errors in thinking and, consequently, focus on skills training and anger management. Critics of this approach argue that although batterers may explain their violence as a result of anger, domestic violence is a deliberate choice to exert power and control over a partner. Anger management, critics say, suggests that the victims share blame by triggering the violence and that batterers are not responsible for their actions because they cannot control them.

Couples therapy is another type of BIP. This model assumes that both parties play a role in the relationship conflict. Proponents say this approach can help keep the family together and is appropriate for less serious domestic violence. But critics assert that couples counseling depends upon openness, flexibility, and the willingness to listen to one another that is not possible when one person is emotionally or physically abusive to the other. Also, it is argued that speaking openly about the abuse invites retaliatory action by the perpetrator, placing the victim at risk for further abuse.

Despite the pitfalls of various BIPs, domestic violence must be addressed. The following viewpoints discuss how these and other prevention strategies are being implemented.

> "The model created by the Duluth Domestic Abuse Intervention Project has been effective."

The Duluth Model of Treatment Is Effective

Stop Violence Against Women

In the following viewpoint, Stop Violence Against Women (SVAW) argues that the so-called Duluth model has been an effective method of batterer intervention in the United States and other countries. The organization maintains that this approach increases victim safety by helping batters acknowledge and end their abusive behavior. According to SVAW, men will not stop battering unless they change the beliefs and attitudes that support the abusive behaviors. Batterers also need training in techniques for controlling anger and addressing conflict without resorting to violence or other forms of abuse. Stop Violence Against Women is an organization dedicated to ending violence against women.

As you read, consider the following questions:

1. What are the three goals of batterer intervention programs, according to SVAW?

Stop Violence Against Women, "Batterers' Intervention Programs," February 1, 2006. www.stopvaw.org. Reproduced by permission.

2. According to the author, class facilitators using the Duluth model challenge men about what attitudes and beliefs?

3. In SVAW's view, what is the relation of batterer intervention programs to marriage or couples counseling?

The purpose of most criminal justice system interventions for domestic violence is to hold the perpetrator accountable for his actions. These interventions, however, are often only a temporary solution to the problem. Even if a perpetrator is sentenced to serve time in prison, his victim may not be any safer when he is released and may even be at greater risk of harm. One approach to increase victim safety is the development of intervention programs designed to help batterers end their abusive behavior. Many batterers' intervention programs have been developed in the United States and Western Europe to help batterers end their violent behavior. Organizations in countries in CEE/FSU [Central and Eastern Europe/Former Soviet Union] are similarly beginning to work with male perpetrators of domestic violence.

Duluth Model Theory

Like other interventions, a batterers' intervention program must be based on a specific theory of violence to be effective. The model created by the Duluth Domestic Abuse Intervention Project has been effective in the United States and has been the basis for several new programs being implemented in countries in CEE/FSU. The Duluth model is based on the theory that violence is intentional and that battering is a system of abusive behaviors that a batterer uses to maintain control over his wife or intimate partner. Other groups have developed different intervention models using this same theory of violence. Batterers' intervention programs, a component of the Duluth coordinated community response model, often give batterers an opportunity to participate in a rehabilitation process in lieu of incarceration....

Batterers Must Take Responsibility

Batterers often minimize their behavior, attributing the abuse to outside factors such as stress at work or alcohol or something their spouse may have done. Until the batterer is willing to accept responsibility for the abuse and recognize that he is always responsible for his actions, no improvement will occur.

United States Conference of Catholic Bishops,
"Batterers and the Sacrament of Reconciliation." www.usccb.org.

There are three goals behind group interventions with batterers: (a) altering beliefs and attitudes toward violence and personal responsibility, (b) planning for safety, and (c) learning alternative skills for nonviolence.

Changing Men's Attitudes

First, batterers' intervention programs work to alter men's beliefs and attitudes toward violence and personal responsibility. Men will not change their behavior by participating in the group unless they are willing to change. Men must recognize and acknowledge their abusive behavior and fully understand the effect it has on their partners, their relationships, and themselves. Men must take responsibility for both the physical violence that they inflict on their partners as well as other forms of abuse such as sexual violence, psychological abuse, and economic coercion. Class facilitators often challenge men about their negative or sexist attitudes and beliefs, support for abusive behaviors, and denial of abuse. This kind of challenge helps men examine the origins of their beliefs and actions with the group and to take responsibility for the abuse.

A second significant goal of a batterers' intervention program is planning for safety. Programs work to support women's safety planning by, for example, developing communication procedures with shelters. Programs can follow these procedures to communicate with shelters when a batterer's behavior in the intervention program indicates a threat to the woman. Programs also refrain from eliciting information from the partners of program participants until the partners have had an opportunity to conduct safety planning.

Teach Batterers Nonviolence Skills

Third, batterers' intervention programs seek to help batterers learn skills for nonviolence. Programs attempt to teach offenders to monitor their actions and to understand the feelings they have when they become violent, such as anger, inadequacy, jealousy, or the need to control the situation. At the same time, however, programs emphasize that while a batterer may feel angry or upset, he must still take personal responsibility for his actions. His use of violence or other forms of abuse is a personal choice.

In helping batterers to learn alternative behaviors, programs may have offenders draw the chain of events that lead to the abusive behaviors. In this way, programs attempt to help batterers to know when they are acting abusively and to recognize warning signs or cues that, for example, indicate that their anger is escalating and that they may become violent. If necessary, the batterers should temporarily withdraw from a situation of conflict. They should talk to someone who will support them in not using violence. When the batterer can react in a non-abusive manner, he should return to discuss the problem without using violence or other forms of abuse. As the intervention program continues, batterers should better understand their abusive behavior and develop alternative skills and methods of interacting with their partners that do not involve violence.

Group Therapy for Batterers

This Duluth model intervention program teaches and reinforces non-violent behavior. It is based on a few guiding principles. First, the program focuses on the safety of the victim and children. Second, it works to hold the perpetrator, not the victim, accountable for his abusive behavior and for stopping the abuse. Third, the program respects the victim's choices and ability to direct her own life. Although some batterers may express regret about their actions, they also receive mixed messages from society that may support their abuse of women. Ideally, a batterers' intervention group provides an environment where men who batter can support each other in non-violent behavior.

The group format provides men with a variety of models and resources to learn how to interact differently with their partners and to change their behavior. Taking part in a program may also help batterers to decrease their dependence on their partners, reduce some of the shame that may come from discussing their abusive behaviors, and help them take responsibility for their actions. Although batterers' intervention classes often take place in a group setting, individual sessions may also be necessary, or helpful, for many men.

The classes are not the same as marriage or couples counseling. Batterers' intervention programs focus on stopping the perpetrator's criminal conduct rather than keeping the couple together. Similarly, they are not substance abuse counseling. Treatment for alcohol and drug abuse should be addressed separately.

> *"'[Batterer intervention programs] based on the Duluth model offer little in terms of rehabilitation and/or prevention of recidivism."*

The Duluth Model of Treatment Is Not Effective

Shawn T. Smith

In the following viewpoint, Shawn T. Smith argues that research shows that the Duluth model is ineffective in preventing domestic violence. The Duluth approach, he maintains, does not lead to lasting changes in the batterers' attitudes and ignores other important factors that contribute to domestic violence. Research shows that causes of domestic violence are better explained by examining individual characteristics of the parties involved rather than blaming violence on societal attitudes about women, he adds. Shawn T. Smith practices psychology in Denver, Colorado.

As you read, consider the following questions:

1. According to a study quoted by Smith, by what percentage do current BIPs reduce the likelihood of repeated incidents of assault by batterers?

Shawn T. Smith, "It's Time for Domestic Violence Treatment to Grow Up," IronShrink .com, November 3, 2006. Reproduced by permission.

2. According to the author, what important factors in domestic violence does the Duluth model tend to ignore?

3. According to Smith, what role does the Duluth model ascribe to examination of couple dynamics?

Research is beginning to suggest that BIPs [batterer intervention programs] based on the Duluth model offer little in terms of rehabilitation and/or prevention of recidivism. In a meta-analytic review, [J.C.] Babcock et al examined the impact of current BIPs based on the Duluth model, cognitive-behavioral interventions, and other methods. They found that "effects due to treatment were in the small range, meaning that the current interventions have a minimal impact on reducing recidivism beyond the effect of being arrested."

Babcock also pointed out that there was no significant difference between Duluth type interventions and Cognitive Behavioral interventions, noting the similarity in content and approach. In comparing this type of treatment against incarceration alone, the authors noted that, "to a clinician, [the low success rate of the Duluth model] means that a woman is 5% less likely to be re-assaulted by a man who was arrested, sanctioned, and went to a batterers' program than by a man who was simply arrested and sanctioned."

Attitude and Behavior Not Changed

According to a study by the National Institute of Justice (NIJ), BIPs based on the Duluth model "do not change batterers' attitudes and may have only minor effects on behavior." NIJ noted studies indicating that offenders who completed a 26-week program had fewer follow-up complaints lodged against them than those who only completed eight weeks of treatment, but was quick to point out that such studies were likely to be confounded by the pre-existing motivation of men who were able to complete a 26-week course. Even then, according to the study, the differences were not statistically significant. . . .

The Duluth model is predicated on the notion that changing attitudes will change behavior. The NIJ study noted that "six months after adjudication, those in the experimental [Duluth model] group saw the woman as slightly less responsible [for his violent behavior]. Even so, the men in the experimental group still viewed their partners as 'somewhat' or 'equally' responsible for the incident." NIJ suggested that current BIPs appear to suppress violent behavior for the duration of treatment, but do not appear to lead to lasting changes in behavior.

In fact, one study based in Broward County, Florida suggested that mandatory treatment based on the Duluth model may have a paradoxically negative effect: "Other things being equal, those assigned to the experimental [Duluth model] group were 2.8 times more likely to be cited for VOPs [violations of parole] than those in the control group."

By way of explaining such lackluster results, NIJ suggested two possibilities: "One is that the evaluations were methodologically flawed; the other is that the design of the programs themselves may be flawed. These two explanations are not necessarily mutually exclusive."

What Are the Dynamics of Violence?

In light of such evidence, the limited scope and empirically untested theoretical framework of the Duluth model are troubling. Some authors have suggested that the treatment of family violence perpetrators has taken place in the absence of empirical data or scientific inquiry, and this appears to be the case with Duluth model treatment.

The authors of the Duluth model explained that the curriculum was defined by the question, "what do the women who have lived through the nightmare of being battered want us to do in these groups?" If the goal of BIPs is to reduce recidivism rates, a more useful question would be, "what are the dynamics that lead to violence in a given intimate relation-

Treatment Is Ideologically Driven

Current treatment strategies are based on the Duluth model, which depicts domestic violence as a function of patriarchy and men's patriarchal privilege. This model assumes that the reason men physically abuse women is to maintain control over them. In ideologically-driven classes for offenders, men in need of serious psychological intervention are instead screamed at and called "domestic terrorists" and "fascists."

Glen Sacks,
"Domestic Violence Treatment Policies Put Abused
Women in Harm's Way," 2005. www.glennsacks.com.

ship?" The former question may be more satisfying to those with an eye toward punishing men in general, but the latter has the advantage of questioning the context, history, and function of violent behavior. And the latter question, by definition, requires empirical research to find the answer. The Duluth model is based not on empiricism but on the feelings and opinion of a politically-charged committee comprised largely of lay people.

Factors Relevant to Domestic Violence

As such, BIPs based on the Duluth model tend to ignore important factors related to violence, including substance abuse, stake-in-conformity motivations, personality features of the batterer, relational dynamics within the couple, history of trauma, and the role of shame.

Substance abuse: [B.] Dalton found that substance abuse was a reliable predictor of treatment program failure—even more reliable than legal threats. [W.] Fals-Stewart found that the chances of violence were eleven times higher during days when the batterer consumed alcohol. Clearly, substance abuse problems are an important factor in domestic violence. Recall that Duluth model programs specifically screen out clients with substance abuse problems.

Stake-in-conformity: Dalton noted that unemployment is a significant predictor of treatment failure. NIJ noted that stake-in-conformity variables such as marital status, residential stability and unemployment are crucial factors in treatment success. Men who are more socially invested tend to have higher success rates in treatment. The Duluth model does not address social investment.

Personality of the batterer: Those who commit crimes of domestic violence (both males and females) score higher on antisocial, aggressive-sadistic, and narcissistic scales on one factor loading, and schizoid, avoidant, and self-defeating scales on a second factor loading. [B.D.] Blanchard noted that: "Narcissism was found to be related to a higher incidence of both minor and total psychological aggression. For the outward expression of anger, there was a main effect for narcissism and an interaction effect for [high] narcissism and [low] self-esteem." The Duluth model does not account, or even allow for, individual differences in personality or motivation.

Relational dynamics: Resmaa Menakem, a researcher with the Tubman Family Alliance in Minneapolis, is one of many researchers who believes that the education model unwisely ignores family dynamics. He explained, "most domestic violence organizations don't know how and don't want to deal with couple dynamics. . . . Their line of thinking is that when you begin to do that, you have to blame the victim. . . . You don't have to give the offender a pass for his violence." Problem solving strategies, which can be ideally developed in a couple treatment modality, might be one key to reducing violence among men who do not pose an immediate threat to their spouses. [J.J.] Schmidt noted that ". . . men who endorsed higher levels of perceived masculine gender role stress, a tendency to attribute more hostile intentions to the partner, and who favored emotion-focused coping over problem-focused coping skills were those most likely to batter." Despite such evidence, the Duluth model specifically prescribes against a systemic approach to ending violent behavior.

History of trauma: Both male and female perpetrators report significantly higher experiences of personal trauma than the general population. The Duluth model views the discussion of personal history as "collusion" with the batterer's violent behavior. Ignoring the connection between personal history and individual violence is, in this author's opinion, shamefully short-sighted and dangerous.

Role of shame: Many researchers have drawn a connection between shame and violence. [J.L.] Jennings & [C.M.] Murphy believe shame and humiliation to be pivotal in male battering behavior. They hypothesized that because of different communication styles and cultural influences, women frequently don't understand when they are humiliating men, and that men who lack communication skills have difficulty knowing how to respond to unintentional humiliation. This is perhaps another argument for couple interventions when deemed safe and appropriate, although [Virginia]Goldner advocates working with individuals "at the level of shame with its connection to violence." Numerous forensic clients have informed this author (and common sense suggests) that the Duluth model is a shame-inducing modality that may actually increase the odds of recidivism.

Duluth Theory Flawed

Researchers are beginning to confirm what common sense dictates: that violence between individuals, while influenced by social and cultural variables such as those cited in the Duluth model, is more parsimoniously explained by an examination of individual characteristics, contexts, and functions of behavior. Not surprisingly, empirical research is beginning to identify shame, individual stressors such as substance abuse and trauma history, and personality characteristics as main contributors to violent behavior in intimate relationships. These findings, combined with the lack of demonstrable success of currently accepted BIPs, call into question the theoretical framework and treatment approach of programs based on the Duluth method.

> "The [domestic violence victims] ... responded [to follow-up questionnaires] by rating the second responders very highly."

Second Responder Programs Are Effective

The Police Foundation

In the following viewpoint, The Police Foundation, analyzing a study of the second responder program in Richmond, Virginia, argues that second responders make victims feel safer and may reduce repeat instances of domestic violence. Police working with second responders, the foundation asserts, provide—and are perceived to provide—better services than police working alone. In the view of the foundation, the study demonstrates that victims of domestic violence support second responder programs. The Police Foundation promotes innovation and improvements in law enforcement in police departments throughout the United States.

As you read, consider the following questions:

1. According to figures quoted by The Police Foundation, in what percentage of cases did second responders assess the safety of members of the household and refer them to the Family Violence Prevention program?

The Police Foundation, "Richmond's Second Responders: Partnering with Police Against Domestic Violence," March 2005, pp. 5–13. www.policefoundation.org. Reproduced by permission.

2. What percentage of domestic violence victims felt the second responders really wanted to help, according to the author?

3. What percentage of victims who received second responder services were very satisfied with the way police handled their situation, compared with those in the control group who did not receive such services, according to The Police Foundation?

The second responders of Richmond are employed by the Department of Social Services (DSS) and based in the first and second of Richmond's four police precincts. This arrangement allows them to interact informally with police officers and participate frequently in roll call. They are on call all night and are summoned to the scene of domestic violence by 911 dispatchers or by patrol officers who respond to domestic violence incidents. After determining the nature of the problem, the second responders go into action and join the police at the site of the call. Assuming the crisis has passed by the time they arrive, the police are supposed to be free to leave and answer other calls.

What Second Responders Do

The second responders begin by ensuring the safety of the victim and her family and assessing the services they need. Then they usually give the victim information on the types of assistance available from the DSS and other agencies, help her develop a plan to receive a range of appropriate services, and ask her to sign a service application form. Second responders may provide victims with short-term emergency shelter, such as hotel rooms, or they may locate and contact support systems. They may also provide food and baby supplies, transportation to safe locations, and bus tickets for travel to and from the DSS and/or court. Second responders, moreover, are knowledgeable about city services and programs related to domestic violence, so they can provide victims with extensive information about protective orders, courts, legal aid, battered women's shelters, and counseling.

Referrals come the next morning to Richmond's Family Violence Prevention Program—located within the DSS—which checks whether the victim already has a caseworker. If so, the caseworker is advised to expand services. Victims who signed a service application will receive a telephone call or visit from a family violence worker within seventy-two hours. Those who didn't will get a letter that provides literature and tells them that services are available when they are ready. . . .

It is important to bear in mind that second responder intervention was triggered only in cases where police had been called and generally when there was probable cause that an assault had occurred, leading to an arrest, an arrest warrant, and/or a protective order. Any intervention by the second responders was in addition to a conventional police response that involved a relatively high degree of legal action. The impact of the second responders on victims therefore supplemented that already made by the police.

Services Provided

To determine what the second responders did, we developed a list of more than twenty services that might be provided, depending on the situation. We asked the members of our treatment group whether the social workers who came to their homes performed the services on the list and if they provided any additional assistance. We also tried to find out if the police performed any of these services or if the woman was unclear who had provided a particular form of assistance.

The women responded to our questions by reporting that they received a variety of services with considerable frequency. In over 75 percent of cases, the women said that the second responder assessed the safety of the members of their household and referred them to the Family Violence Prevention Program. In over 60 percent of cases, the second responder

Not Just a Law Enforcement Problem

The collaborative approach to family violence recognizes that crime problems and their effects on victims are not solely a law enforcement matter. Through the formation of partnerships, typically within the context of community policing, a comprehensive, coproductive approach to family violence is currently viewed as a promising way to reduce the occurrence of family violence.

Andrew L. Giacomazzi and Martha Smithey,
"A Collaborative Effort Toward Resolving Family Violence
Against Women," National Criminal Justice Reference Service, 2004.

talked with the woman about her general legal rights and specifically discussed protective orders and services available from the DSS. In over half of the cases, the second responder gave the woman information about going to court, as well as discussing where she and her family could stay. Then the second responder frequently provided legal and practical information. . . .

Women Favor Second Responders

We asked the women a number of specific questions to assess their attitudes toward the second responders. We were interested in exploring such issues as: How carefully did the second responders listen to your side? How seriously did the second responders take your situation? Did the second responders seem like they really wanted to help? How useful were the second responders in helping you deal with your problem? How strongly would you recommend the second responders? And, finally, how satisfied were you with the second responders?

The women generally responded by rating the second responders very highly. . . . Eighty-eight percent, for example, felt that the second responders listened very carefully to their stories; 82 percent believed that the second responders took their situation very seriously; and 92 percent felt that the second responders really wanted to help. Seventy-three percent were very satisfied with their general encounter with the second responders, and 79 percent indicated that they would very strongly recommend the second responders to someone else in their situation. Granted, only 51 percent considered the second responders to be very useful in helping them resolve problems relating to their intimate partners, but this lower score may reflect domestic issues that are not amenable to resolution within the limited contact between second responders and their clients.

This possible shortfall did not deter most of the women from singing the praises of the second responders in chats with the researchers. A minority voiced some dissatisfaction with the service and advice they received; a few even felt that the second responders were interfering. Most of the women, however, were grateful to the social workers for taking time with them, listening to their stories, making them feel safer, and providing comfort to them and their children. . . .

Second Responders Improve Police Services

Women who received second responder treatment also got better service from police, as shown by their reaction to a list of services—many the same as those performed by second responders—that officers might provide. The women's responses to our questionnaires helped us compare the performance of police working in conjunction with second responders with that of police working alone. The remarks they made in interviews further fleshed out our picture of the services received by victims of domestic violence, whether they came from the police alone, as in the control group, or from police and second responders, as in the treatment group.

The responses of the two groups showed that some of the increase in service to the treatment group was in areas to which police might have been sensitized by the presence of the second responders. For example, 41 percent of treatment subjects, as compared to 3 percent of control subjects, reported that police referred them to the DSS; and 30 percent of the treatment group, as compared to 4 percent of the control group, reported that police discussed the services available from the DSS.

More intriguing was the general perception that traditional police services were also enhanced by the presence of second responders. For example, 74 percent of the treatment group, compared with 53 percent of the control group, said that police assessed their safety and that of others; and 64 percent of the treatment group, compared with 37 percent of the control group, said that police talked with them about obtaining protective orders. In fact, . . . women in the treatment group received more of all services pertaining to legal aspects of their situation—whether it be discussing protective orders or referring them to legal services—though these activities are a normal part of the traditional police response. . . .

These reported differences in police service to the two groups translated into a predictably higher opinion of the police within the treatment group. Perhaps most telling was the difference in the level of overall satisfaction, with 64 percent of the treatment group, compared with 38 percent of the control group, being very satisfied with the way police handled their situation. . . .

Revictimization Reduced

To determine whether the Second Responder Program actually reduced victimization, we began by testing for differences in the prevalence of the four individual items. As we observed, women who received second responder services were less likely to report each form of abuse—physical harm, threat of physical harm, threat to kill, and property damage—than women in the control group. Twenty percent of the women in the treatment group, ... reported some form of victimization compared to 35 percent of women in the control group, a difference of marginal statistical significance. ...

We continued our analysis by examining the incidence of abusive acts in the periods before and after intervention. By summing up the number of acts reported in the individual categories by each study participant, we were able to make the following comparison of the two groups. There were only minimal differences in the period before intervention, when women in the control group reported a mean number of 14.88 abusive acts, and the treatment group reported 13.62. Substantial differences appeared, however, six months after intervention, when members of the control group reported a mean number of 12.42 acts, while members of the treatment group reported only 2.30. Moreover, a multivariate test, controlling for pre-arrest levels of abuse, also found differences between the two groups six months after the triggering incident.

> *"The best available evidence suggests that [second responder] programs are at best ineffective and at worst may place victims in greater harm."*

Second Responder Programs Are Not Effective

Robert C. Davis, David Weisburd, and Edwin E. Hamilton

In the following viewpoint, Robert C. Davis, David Weisburd, and Edwin E. Hamilton argue that second responder programs are not effective in addressing domestic violence. The authors, analyzing the results of their study of the Redlands, California, second responder program, maintain that second responder intervention does not reduce the potential for future abuse. In fact, the evidence suggests, acording to the authors, that intervention by second responders increases the likelihood of abuse. Robert C. Davis, David Weisburd, and Edwin E. Hamilton are researchers in the field of criminal justice.

As you read, consider the following questions:

1. What question did the Redlands, California, study set out to test, according to the authors?

Robert C. Davis, David Weisburd, and Edwin E. Hamilton, "Preventing Repeat Incidents of Family Violence: A Randomized Field Test of a Second Responder Program in Redlands, CA," U.S. Department of Justice, August 20, 2007.

2. What do Davis, Weisburd, and Hamiltion say is the difference in the rate of recidivism between those receiving second responder services and those not receiving such services?

3. How many of the seven principal outcomes measured in the authors' study showed a reduction in abuse in favor of the groups that received second responder services?

It is no longer assumed that the initial patrol response to domestic incidents—especially those incidents where no arrest is made—is sufficient in and of itself to protect victims from recurrence of abuse. Domestic violence experts have come to realize that effective solutions to domestic violence must involve efforts to educate victims about their options and connect them with counseling, relocation, civil legal assistance, and other services that can lessen dependence on the abuser. In recent years a number of programs have been developed in which social workers ("second responders") visit homes in which domestic incidents were recently reported to the police in order to help them find long-term solutions to recurring abuse. While these programs rapidly gained in popularity in the United States, the evidence regarding their effectiveness is mixed. Although some research has indicated that second responder programs can prevent repeat victimization, the most rigorous studies have suggested that these programs may actually increase the odds of abuse recurring.

Mixed Results

A study by the Police Foundation and a Portland, OR, study by [A.] Jolin, et al both had suggested that second response programs reduce future abuse as measured by victim reports in surveys. But there were difficulties interpreting the results of both studies. The Police Foundation study was a quasi-experiment, and it was clear that the cases chosen for a second response by the Richmond Police Department were a small fraction of all cases eligible according to the study's criteria: How the cases were assigned was not known or not reported by the researchers. The Jolin study randomly assigned cases to treatments, but confounded second responses with collection of additional evidence by the police that resulted in more case filings, more convictons, and tougher sentences. It is unknown whether it was the second response or the enhanced criminal justice outcomes that were responsible for the observed decrease in subsequent abuse reported by victims.

A series of studies in New York were specifically designed to test the effects of second response programs using true experimental designs, the "gold standard" in research methodologies. A pooled analysis conducted by [R.C.] Davis, et al reanalyzed data from three separate field experiments, each testing the same intervention on somewhat different populations. The pooled analyses consistently indicated that the interventions were associated with an increase in reporting of new abusive incidents not only to authorities, but also to research interviewers. The New York field tests suggested that second response programs might actually increase the likelihood of new abuse.

Method for this Study

The Redlands, California, field trial assessed one parameter of second response programs that might account for the variation in research findings. Based on a supposition that victims may be especially receptive to crime prevention opportunities immediately following victimization the Redlands study set out to test the question of whether more efficacious outcomes would be gained the closer that a second response occurs to the actual domestic violence event. Accordingly, the field test included three levels of timing of a second responder intervention: immediate, delayed, or none. The study employed a randomized experimental design. Such designs, when properly designed and implemented, are generally agreed to provide the highest level of confidence in drawing policy conclusions.

From the study, we hoped to identify whether there are versions of this intervention that are likely to reduce continuing abuse and whether there are versions that have no effect or actually increase abuse. We hoped that the results would affect how criminal justice planners, victim service providers, and law enforcement agencies design and implement these programs.

The study was conducted in Redlands, California, a community of 70,000 at the foot of the mountains and edge of the desert in the East Valley region of southwest San Bernardino County. With the cooperation of the Redlands, CA, Police Department, we conducted a randomized experiment in which households that reported a domestic incident to the police were assigned to one of three experimental conditions: (a) second responders were dispatched to the crime scene within 24 hours; (b) second responders visited victims' homes one week after the call for service; or (c) no second response occurred. . . .

No Difference in Rate of Recidivism

The data shows that the one-day response group generated somewhat more new incidents (32 percent) compared to the seven-day response group (23 percent) or the control group (24 percent). The two second response groups combined yielded a 28 percent rate of new incidents compared to the control group rate of 24 percent. None of these differences approached statistical significance. We also analyzed separately only those new incidents that were known to involve the same perpetrator as the original incident. Those results, . . . showed essentially no difference according to treatment groups. . . .

Victim Interviews

Victims in the second response groups were somewhat more likely to report having seen the abuser since the original inci-

Intervention Can Increase Danger

A victim of domestic violence who has left the abuser or is seeking counseling which may lead to the victim leaving the abuser is at an even higher risk of harm. Social workers must understand that even the fact that a victim is telling an outsider the "family secrets" poses a risk. Any threat to the abuser's control, especially the threat of the victim leaving the abuser, can escalate the abuser's violence.

Christine Heer,
"Ethical Issues in Domestic Violence," Social Work Today,
November/December 2006. www.socialworktoday.com.

dent. Ninety-seven percent of those assigned to the one-day response reported having seen the abuser compared to 91 percent of those assigned to the seven-day response condition and 84 percent of those assigned to the control condition. This difference did not approach statistical significance in a test run combining both second response conditions.

[Regarding] differences between the treatment groups in new abusive incidents, on all of the measures—from physical abuse to threats to controlling abuse to total abuse—victims assigned to the second response conditions were somewhat more likely than those assigned to the control condition to respond affirmatively. The difference was slight for incidents of physical abuse (9 percent versus 7 percent), but more substantial when all forms of abuse were taken into account (45 percent versus 31 percent). However, none of the differences reached statistical significance.

Second Response Did Not Reduce Abuse

The Redlands study was designed as a test of the second responder model with a population not from a major metropolitan area. It also varied the timing of the response, one factor thought to potentially affect the efficacy of the intervention. The study yielded no evidence that the intervention helped reduce the potential for subsequent abuse. Not one of the seven principal outcomes measured (prevalence and frequency of new abuse; time to failure; survey measures of physical abuse, threats, and controlling abuse; and satisfaction with the police response) showed a reduction in abuse in favor of the groups that received the second response.

In fact, the evidence suggests—although certainly not definitively—that the intervention increased abusive incidents. The difference in the prevalence of any abusive incident reported on the survey was substantial (14 percentage points higher for those assigned to the second response conditions than for controls) although not statistically reliable with the available sample size. On all seven principal measures of new abuse, second response cases performed worse than controls.

It would be difficult to argue that the failure of the field test to yield positive results was caused by poor implementation of the program. In a very high proportion of households assigned to receive a second response, face-to-face interviews were conducted with the victim. There were checks on the integrity of the intervention, including completion of a checklist by the officers conducting the second responses to indicate that all key areas were touched upon in their discussion with victims. Members of the research staff also conducted ridealongs at several points during the study to ensure that the protocol was being followed. Finally, an overwhelming proportion of victims indicated that they found the visits helpful.

Intervention May Increase Abuse

We cannot say for certain why the field test did not yield more positive results. We have some indication that intimate partners who found out about the intervention were more likely to commit new abuse. If so, then any beneficial effects that the intervention might have in educating victims or encouraging them to seek help may have been offset by a hostile response to the intervention by abusers. Both [J.A.] Fagan and [L.W.] Sherman warn that criminal sanctions may incite more abuse, especially among the chronic abusers or those with low stakes in conformity. In the same vein, [D.A.] Ford reports results from an experiment that batterers who were prosecuted to conviction were significantly angrier than men whose cases were diverted or dropped.

The results of this field test, when considered in the light of the results of the New York experiments, should send up a strong caution signal to those funding and those implementing second response programs. The best available evidence suggests that these programs are at best ineffective and at worst may place victims in greater harm.

> *"There are very few functions of the judicial branch where you can point and say, 'This is saving lives.'... [Tightening restraining order rules] is one of them."*

Enforcing Restraining Orders Will Curb Domestic Violence

Tania Chatila

In the following viewpoint, Tania Chatila argues that better enforcement of restraining orders will improve protection against domestic violence. The author describes the shooting deaths of two women who had obtained restraining orders against their assailants, noting that the law prohibits those with restraining orders filed against them from possessing firearms. Judges, she notes, do not always include the firearm prohibition in the order. Improvements to the databases used to keep track of restraining orders are also needed, she maintains. While improvements in implementation of restraining orders have occurred, the author contends that more is needed. Tania Chatila writes for the Pasadena Star-News *in California.*

Tania Chatila "Report Backs Tightening of Restraining Order Rules," *Pasadena Star-News*, March 1, 2008. Copyright © 2007 Los Angeles Newspaper Group. Reproduced by permission of the *Pasadena Star-News*.

As you read, consider the following questions:

1. Why, according to Chatila, are firearm prohibitions not always included in restraining orders?
2. According to the author, how does California's Safe at Home program protect the identity of domestic abuse victims who must provide addresses for public purposes?
3. According to the author, what caused the police to arrest a woman in Pomona, California, who, fearing for her life, obtained a temporary restraining order?

A dvocates for victims of domestic violence hope recommendations to tighten restraining order rules will improve protection for abuse victims.

California's judicial council [in February 2008] recommended better enforcement of firearm prohibitions, the creation of a statewide system to view scanned copies of all restraining orders and increased efficiency in the state's existing Domestic Violence Restraining Order System database, known as DVROS.

The proposals are among 139 guidelines. That report took more than two years to complete and stems from an attorney general's task force formed in 2003 to examine how state agencies respond to domestic violence cases.

"There are very few functions of the judicial branch where you can point and say, 'This is saving lives,'" said Laurence Donald Kay, chair of the Domestic Violence Practice and Procedure Task Force. "This is one of them."

Failure to Enforce Costs Lives

Following the recent deaths of [local area residents] Monica Thomas-Harris and Ana Maria Acosta, experts and advocacy groups have questioned why so little legal protection appeared to be available to either woman.

Restraining Orders Can Be Effective

Restraining orders can be a powerful tool to prevent batterers from committing further domestic violence, so long as there is a credible threat that violators will be sanctioned.

Both Criminal and Family Courts have authority to issue these restraining orders:

- Criminal Courts must issue a Criminal Protective Order (CPO) when sentencing a domestic violence defendant to probation (the typical sentence). Such an order either prohibits the offender from having contact with the victim, or requires the offender to have peaceful contact with the victim (often issued if they still live together or share child custody).

- Family Courts must issue a restraining order, in the form of a Temporary Restraining Order or a permanent Order After Hearing, if the victim offers "reasonable proof" of domestic violence. Like a CPO, such an order either prohibits contact or requires peaceful contact.

- All such orders must prohibit firearms possession, and must direct the abuser to surrender any firearms within 24 hours.

Report to California Attorney General from the Task Force on Local Criminal Justice Response to Domestic Violence, June 2005. http://safestate.org.

"I absolutely think anything you can do to tighten the system up is going to be a benefit," said Kim Plater, a vice president of the Covina Woman's Club and a member of the club's Domestic Violence Action Committee. "It's more of a tool for the judges and a tool to the judicial system."

Thomas-Harris, 37, of Upland was shot by her estranged husband, Curtis Bernard Harris, on Jan. 5 before he turned the gun on himself. Acosta's estranged husband, Aaron Raigoza, was arrested Thursday in the shooting death of Acosta, 32, of Monterey Park on Feb. 4.

Prior to their deaths, both women had filed for temporary restraining orders against their spouses, indicating abuse.

Such orders need more teeth, said Laura Avina, Acosta's sister.

"If there is more enforcement, it might help," she said. "But as far as the system is right now, a restraining order really isn't going to do anything. I think there just needs to be more protection."

Orders Must Prohibit Firearms

Kay said the recommendations intend to provide that protection.

"This report intends not only to raise awareness and focus priorities of the California courts to the epidemic of domestic violence," he said, "but also to encourage adoption of recommendations that will make implementation easier."

For example, current law dictates that anyone with a restraining order filed against them cannot be in possession of a firearm. A reference to this is made on California restraining order forms.

But those prohibitions are not always enforced, Kay said.

"It's true we have encountered situations in which judges have either not used the California form or when they are using the form, they have drawn a line through the gun restrictions," he said.

Kay hopes the report will help enforce this "necessary" prohibition at the judicial and law enforcement levels, so that judges follow legislation and police confiscate weapons immediately.

Restraining Order Database Improvements

He also said officials need to better maintain the DVROS database. He touted the report's proposal to create a secured statewide system that would allow police, judges and court employees access to scanned images of active restraining orders in California.

A prototype is already up and running in Orange County, he said.

"There is always room for improvement in terms of the system and the restraining order system," said Olivia Rodriguez, executive director of the Domestic Violence Council of Los Angeles County.

She had not seen the task force report Friday, but said the "attorney general's office seems to be doing some excellent work in the domestic violence area."

Today's system has actually improved by leaps and bounds compared to years ago, said Hermine Honarvar-Rule, an attorney with Community Legal Services in Norwalk.

She pointed to dozens of clinics and programs for abuse victims, and the state's Safe at Home program, which provides victims with mailing addresses so they don't have to use home addresses on public forms.

"It's not all doom and gloom," Honarvar-Rule said. "In my field of work, I've seen great improvements."

An Order Saved Her Life

Maria—a domestic violence victim from La Puente who asked not to be identified by her full name out of fear for her life—attested to those improvements.

She was granted a temporary restraining order against her boyfriend, Philip Valin, 35, of Pomona, who she claims sexually assaulted her. Valin was arrested after violating the order.

Kay was confident implementation of the recommendations—no matter how much or how difficult—would help.

"This is going to take a lot of work," he said. "It's going to cost money to save lives. But whatever it is, we are going to have to come up with it."

> *"[Restraining orders] are only a piece of paper, so alleged victims . . . need to protect themselves in any way they can. . . . [The] police can't be with them 24 hours a day."*

Restraining Orders Cannot Prevent Some Domestic Violence

Emily Kittle

In the following viewpoint, Emily Kittle argues that while many perpetrators of domestic violence obey restraining orders, others repeatedly violate them. Often, she says, victims later will want restraining orders dropped or modified but repeated violations can be grounds for keeping the order in place. She cites instances of perpetrators violating an order, being arrested, and violating it again hours later. While the consequences to perpetrators for violating restraining orders—additional jail time—can be serious, she notes, the consequences to victims can be fatal. Emily Kittle writes for the Telegraph-Herald *newspaper in Dubuque, Iowa.*

As you read, consider the following questions:

1. Why, according to a prosecutor cited by Kittle, are no-contact orders helpful when someone is arrested after an argument?

2. Why in some cases, according to the victim-witness co-ordinator quoted by the author, might a victim be better off without a no-contact order?

3. What percentage of perpetrators violate no-contact orders in Dubuque county, according to the prosecutor quoted by the Kittle?

Even behind bars, Caine Meek reportedly tried to defy a judge's order.

In jail awaiting trial for attempted murder, the 23-year-old man secretly tried to make contact with the woman he had badly beaten with a metal pipe in front of their four children, according to law enforcement officials.

After being court-ordered to have no contact with Che'Navia Conley, Meek allegedly tried to get around the system by asking a fellow Dubuque County Jail inmate's girlfriend to relay a message to the woman. He reportedly wanted Conley to write to him, going as far as requesting that she pen the letter under an alias to avoid detection.

The covert effort failed, and Meek was charged with violating his no-contact order, on top of a host of charges he faced in connection with the attack....

As a result of plea negotiations, the no-contact order violation charge later was dismissed, as was the attempted-murder charge. Meek received a 25-year prison sentence after pleading guilty to other charges he faced in connection with the attack that hospitalized Conley with numerous injuries.

Orders Work for Many

Meek didn't succeed in his alleged attempt to contact his victim. Some offenders do, however, perhaps underscoring that restraining orders ultimately are nothing more than a piece of paper. But law enforcement officials say the prevalent protective orders, for the most part, are an effective tool in keeping offenders away from their victims.

"I think that the majority of people, when the judge issues an order and says you cannot contact that person, abide by that order," Dubuque Police Capt. Scott Crabill said. "(But) there are those who don't abide by the order and have been arrested multiple times for violating the same order."

Dubuque police [in 2005] opened 168 investigations into reports of violations of no-contact orders, many of which included the same offenders. Sixty percent of those cases resulted in an arrest. Police [in 2006] investigated 149 no-contact order violation complaints.

No Contact Guidelines

Typically, when a suspect is charged with a domestic-related crime, a judge issues an order barring contact between the defendant and named victim as a condition of bond.

"When someone is arrested, emotions are high, and the first thing they want to do is go back there and continue the argument," said Assistant Dubuque County Attorney Bob Richter, who prosecutes domestic abuse cases. "No-contact orders tend to de-escalate the situation a little bit."

And no contact means no contact.

Dubuque County District Court Associate Judge Randal Nigg, who handles domestic abuse cases on a daily basis, can recite by heart the lengthy list of restrictions he walks each defendant through. The directives encompass the most finite forms of contact, from text messages to e-mails to third-party contact, like Meek was accused of trying.

"We're trying to establish a very bright line for these folks, so it's clear that they are to have no contact, and that no means no," the judge said.

Orders Can Be a Catalyst for Violence

To the person who has no respect for the order of the court or the rule of law, the person most likely to kill an estranged spouse or lover, the restraining order is "just a piece of paper"—a catalyst, perhaps, to commit the ultimate violent act against someone that person once loved and cherished.

Kathleen Mercer, Eugene (OR) Register-Guard, *January 2, 2006.*

In addition to the no-contact guidelines, defendants who possess firearms are required under federal law to surrender their weapons for safekeeping. The no-contact order is in effect for the life of the defendant's case, unless the court sees fit to modify the mandate, and can be renewed in five-year increments upon request.

Restoring Contact

Most victims, at some point, do want the protection order modified or dropped altogether, according to Julie Homb, victim-witness coordinator with the Dubuque County Attorney's Office. But before the prosecutor's office requests the court to change an order, the victim usually is asked to meet with an advocate and put together a safety plan, used in the event of a volatile issue.

Contact between the parties might be gradually restored. For instance, the offender and victim might first be allowed to contact each other by letter, then by phone and eventually face-to-face.

"They're real people with real lives and real hopes and dreams," Homb said of domestic abuse victims. "We're not here to control their lives; we're just trying to work with them to keep their lives more manageable, and above all to keep them safe."

Some Violate Orders Repeatedly

Restoring contact between individuals is not always feasible though. A Dubuque County judge denied one victim's request to vacate a no-contact order between her and the father of her children.

"In this case alone, there have been seven violations of the no-contact order, and there have been new assaults while the protective order was in place," Dubuque County District Court Associate Judge Richard Gleason wrote in the order. "It is the court's opinion that both of these individuals need separate counseling for as long as possible if there is any chance that they can resume a non-violent relationship."

The named defendant, 25-year-old Robert D. Smith, of Dubuque, most recently was arrested in front of the woman's residence after he allegedly violated the order again. Court records state that Smith phoned the woman, 26-year-old Rose M. Scott, multiple times and said he was on his way to her home.

Scott notified police, and officers found the man on the sidewalk outside of her home at about 2:30 a.m. Smith reportedly denied having any phone contact with the woman and said he was on his way to a friend's house.

There are cases, though, where the victim might actually be safer without a protection order, according to Homb. The most dangerous time for a domestic abuse victim is when she leaves her perpetrator, Homb said, so a no-contact order can heighten a victim's risk of injury.

In fiscal year 2006, 239 no-contact orders were issued in connection with domestic abuse cases, according to the Dubuque County Attorney's Office. Since July 1, [2006,] 116 of those orders have been directed. Homb estimates that 10 to 20 percent of defendants violate the court orders.

"Most people who violate the order violate it more than one time," she said. "It's like compliance with anything else. Either they're going to be compliant or they're not."

Consequences of Violations

Penalties can be stiff for violators. Police are required to make an immediate arrest if they have probable cause that a violation of a no-contact order was committed. If found guilty in Iowa, the offender faces a minimum of seven days in jail and up to 180 days behind bars.

"We've had offenders get arrested for domestic violence or for violating a no-contact order, and within three or four hours has violated that order and has found himself right back in jail," said Crabill.

And there can be fatal results. Nationally, offenders have violated protective orders and killed their victims.

"They are only a piece of paper, so alleged victims need to be cognizant that they need to protect themselves in any way that they can," Nigg said. "Named victims have an order from the court and have the power of enforcement there, but the police can't be with them 24 hours a day."

Violators Should Be Reported

Homb said the entire community has a stake in making the system work. The victim-witness coordinator said it's up to everyone—from neighbors to strangers to the victims themselves—to take a "social responsibility" in reporting no-contact order violations.

The principle of the restraining order turns the motivation of domestic abuse on its head, Homb said.

"Isolation of the victim from the outside world is a big part of what it takes to be a successful batterer," she said, "and being able to isolate the batterer from the victim for once kind of evens things out and balances the scales for once."

Periodical Bibliography

The following articles have been selected to supplement the diverse views presented in this chapter:

Edward W. Gondolf — "Theoretical and Research Support for the Duluth Model: A Reply to Dutton and Corvo," *Aggression & Violent Behavior*, November–December, 2007.

Jennifer Langhinrichsen-Rohling and John Friend — "Stopping Domestic Violence: Detailing an Integrative Skill-Based Group Approach for Abusive Men," *Psychology of Women Quarterly*, March 2008.

T.K. Logan, Jennifer Cole, Lisa Shannon, and Robert Walker — "Relationship Characteristics and Protective Orders Among a Diverse Sample of Women," *Journal of Family Violence*, May 2007.

Lisa D. May — "The Backfiring of the Domestic Violence Firearms Bans," *Columbia Journal of Gender and Law*, January 1, 2005.

Judy L. Postmas — "Challenging the Negative Assumptions Surrounding Civil Protection Orders," *Affilia: Journal of Women & Social Work*, Winter 2007.

James E. Rivers, Candace L. Maze, Stephanie Hannah, and Cindy S. Lederman — "Domestic Violence Screening and Service Acceptance Among Adult Victims in a Dependency Court Setting," *Child Welfare*, January 1, 2007.

Lisa Shannon, T.K. Logan and Jennifer Cole — "Intimate Partner Violence, Relationship Status, and Protective Orders," *Journal of Interpersonal Violence*, September 2007.

Leonard A. Sipes Jr. — "Domestic Violence Prevention in Washington, D.C.," *Sheriff*, January 1, 2007.

Mandeep Talwar — "Improving the Enforcement of Restraining Orders After *Castle Rock v. Gonzales*," *Family Court Review*, April 2007.

For Further Discussion

Chapter 1

1. Mark S. Kiselica and Mandy Morrill-Richards contend that sibling abuse is a serious but largely unrecognized domestic violence problem. Why do you think this type of domestic violence is less recognized than spousal abuse?

2. Tod W. Burke and Stephen S. Owen argue that same-sex domestic violence is as serious a problem as domestic violence between heterosexual intimate partners. Does this mean that the causes of domestic violence are identical for same-sex couples as they are for heterosexual couples?

3. After reading all of the articles in the chapter, how, if at all, do you think domestic violence among high school and college students differs from the other types of domestic violence discussed in the chapter?

Chapter 2

1. The Minnesota Advocates for Human Rights argues that domestic violence occurs because men want to control women, but Maureen C. Outlaw and Richard B. Felson contend that men are no more controlling than women. Which article presents a more convincing argument and why?

2. Carey Roberts claims women cause more domestic violence than men, but the report from the United Nations Population Fund attributes domestic violence to gender inequality. Can both of these viewpoints be correct? If so, how?

Chapter 3

1. After reading Diane M. Stuart's article on the Violence Against Women Act (VAWA), do you believe the Act is working? Do you believe there would be more or less domestic violence had VAWA never been adopted and implemented?

2. After reading the articles on mandatory arrests by Rasmieyh Abdelnabi and Radha Iyengar, do you think police officers should have discretion in deciding whether to arrest when domestic violence is alleged to have occurred? If police had discretion in these situations, how would they decide when arrest was appropriate?

3. Chapter 3 discusses legistlative treatment of domestic violence cases. Do you think it is possible to be completely fair to men accused of domestic violence and also provide adequate protection to women? If you could change the laws, how would you change them?

Chapter 4

1. The Duluth model of treatment assumes that domestic violence is a choice. Do you think it is? Why or why not?

2. After reading the articles on the Duluth model by Stop Violence Against Women and Shawn T. Smith, what do you think are the pros and cons of the approach taken by the Duluth model?

3. The articles on second responders by The Police Foundation and by Robert C. Davis, David Weisburd, and Edwin E. Hamilton reach different conclusions regarding the program's effectiveness at preventing domestic violence. Should money be spent on second responder programs even if they aren't shown to prevent domestic violence? Why or why not?

4. After reading the articles concerning restraining orders by Tania Chatila and Emily Kittle, do you believe they contribute to preventing domestic violence? What would you do to make them more effective?

Organizations to Contact

The editors have compiled the following list of organizations concerned with the issues debated in this book. The descriptions are derived from materials provided by the organizations. All have publications or information available for interested readers. The list was compiled on the date of publication of the present volume; the information provided here may change. Readers need to remember that many organizations take several weeks or longer to respond to inquiries.

American Bar Association Commission
on Domestic Violence
740 Fifteenth St. NW, Washington, DC 20005
(202) 662-1000
e-mail: abacdv@abanet.org
Web site: www.abanet.org/domviol/home.html

The American Bar Association Commission on Domestic Violence researches violence programs and provides information on domestic violence law. The group also publishes books on domestic violence. The Web site has a searchable database.

Battered Women's Justice Project (BWJP)
1801 Nicollet Ave. S, Suite 102, Minneapolis, MN 55403
(800) 903-0111 • fax: (612) 824-8965
Web site: www.bwjp.org

BWJP is a collaborative effort of three organizations that promote innovative civil and criminal justice responses to domestic violence: the Pennsylvania Coalition Against Domestic Violence, the National Clearinghouse for the Defense of Battered Women, and Minnesota Program Development, Inc. BWJP works to make community organizations and government agencies involved in civil and criminal justice response to domestic violence more accountable for the safety of battered women and their families. BWJP's Web site has articles and information on domestic violence as well as links to other resources.

Family Violence Prevention Fund
383 Rhode Island St., Suite 304
San Francisco, CA   94103-5133
(415) 252-8900
e-mail: info@endabuse.org
Web site: http://endabuse.org

The Family Violence Prevention Fund works to prevent violence in the home and community to help those harmed by violence. It provides education services and promotes progressive policies regarding domestic violence. The group's Web site has domestic violence news and resources.

Independent Women's Forum
1726 M St. NW, Tenth Floor, Washington, DC   20036
(202) 419-1820
e-mail:info@iwf.org
Web site: www.iwf.org

The Independent Women's Forum is a conservative women's advocacy group. The group believes that the incidence of domestic violence is exaggerated and that legislation and programs designed to reduce domestic violence are often excessive and unwarranted. The group's website has articles and research critical of the federal Violence Against Women Act.

Institute on Domestic Violence in the African American Community (IDVAAC)
University of Minnesota, School of Social Work
St. Paul, MN   55108-6142
(877) (643-8222) • fax: (612)-624-9201
e-mail: nidvaac@umn.edu
Web site: www.dvinstitute.org/

The Institute on Domestic Violence in the African American Community (IDVAAC) is an organization focused on the unique circumstances of African Americans as they face issues related to domestic violence, including intimate partner violence, child abuse, elder maltreatment, and community violence. IDVAAC works to enhance society's understanding of and ability to end violence in the African-American community. IDVAAC also works with a variety of partners to build the knowledge base concerning domestic violence and African Americans, and to develop strategies to meet the service needs of this population. The organization's Web site has information about domestic violence, projects of the organization, and links to resources.

National Coalition Against Domestic Violence (NCADV)
1120 Lincoln St., Suite 1603, Denver, CO   80203
(303) 839-1852 • fax: 303-831-9251
Web site: www.ncadv.org

The mission of the National Coalition Against Domestic Violence (NCADV) is to organize various stakeholders to advance transformative policies as well as improve the thinking and leadership of communities and individuals working to end domestic violence. NCADV's work includes coalition building at the local, state, regional, and national levels; support for the provision of community-based, non-violent alternatives—such as safe-home and shelter programs—for battered women and their children; public education and technical assistance; and policy development and innovative legislation. The organization's Web site has news and information on domestic violence.

National Criminal Justice Reference Service (NCJRS)
PO Box 6000, Rockville, MD   20849
(800) 851-3420 • fax: (301) 519-5212
e-mail: askncjrs@ncjrs.org
Web site: www.ncjrs.gov

NCJRS supports and conducts research on crime, criminal behavior, and crime prevention. It also acts as a clearinghouse for criminal justice information worldwide. The agency's searchable Web site contains useful information and reports on domestic violence.

National Network to End Domestic Violence (NNEDV)
660 Pennsylvania Ave. SE, Suite 303, Washington, DC   20003
(202) 543-5566
Web site: www.nnedv.org

The NNEDV represents state domestic violence coalitions. It focuses on legal and legislative activities. The group's Web site describes the programs and projects in which it is involved and provides news about domestic violence and links to domestic violence resources.

Respecting Accuracy in Domestic Abuse Reporting (RADAR)
PO Box 1404, Rockville, MD   20849
email: info@mediaradar.org
Web site: www.mediaradar.org/index.php

RADAR believes that domestic violence statistics are exaggerated, that male victims are underserved, and that current laws unfairly treat men accused of domestic violence. RADAR also believes that the Violence Against Women Act (VAWA) undermines families and should be reformed. RADAR's website has articles and information on domestic violence.

U.S. Department of Justice Office on Violence Against Women
800 K St. NW, Suite 920, Washington, DC   20530
(202) 307-6026 • fax: (202) 307-3911
Web site: www.usdoj.gov/ovw

The U.S. Department of Justice Office on Violence Against Women maintains a National Domestic Violence Hotline and publishes a monthly newsletter on domestic violence. The Web site has press releases, speeches and news about domestic violence as well as an online domestic violence awareness manual.

Bibliography of Books

Jocelyn Andersen — *Women Submit! Christians and Domestic Violence*, Auburndale, FL: One Way Café Press, 2007.

Lundy Bancroft — *When Dad Hurts Mom: Helping Your Children Heal the Wounds of Witnessing Abuse*, New York: G.P. Putnam's Sons, 2004.

Sandra L. Brown — *Family Interventions in Domestic Violence: A Handbook of Gender-Inclusive Theory and Treatment*, New York: Springer, 2007.

Christina M. Dalpiaz — *Breaking Free, Starting Over: Parenting in the Aftermath of Family Violence.* Westport, CN: Praeger, 2004.

Todd Denny — *Unexpected Allies: Men Who Stop Rape*, Victoria, BC, Canada: Trofford Publishing, 2007.

Donald Dutton — *The Abusive Personality: Violence and Control in Intimate Relationships*, New York: Guilford Press, 2007.

Diane Glass — *Stalking the Stalker: Fighting Back with High-Tech Gadgets and Low-Tech Know-How*, New York: iUniverse, 2006.

Marianne Hester, Chris Pearson, Nicola Harwin, and Hillary Abrahams — *Making an Impact: Children and Domestic Violence, a Reader*, Philadelphia: J. Kingsley, 2007.

Denise A. Hines and Kathleen Malley-Morrison
Family Violence in the United States: Defining, Understanding, and Combating Abuse, Thousand Oaks, CA: Sage Publications, 2005.

Richard T. Hise
The War Against Men, Oakland, OR: Elderberry Press, 2004.

Christina Hoff
The War Against Boys: How Misguided Feminism Is Harming Our Young Men, New York: Simon & Schuster, 2004.

Nicky Ali Jackson, ed.
Encyclopedia of Domestic Violence, New York: Routledge, 2007.

Nancy Janovicek
No Place to Go: Local Histories of the Battered Women's Shelter Movement, Seattle, WA: University of Washington Press, 2007.

Jackson Katz
The Macho Paradox: Why Some Men Hurt Women and How All Men Can Help, Naperville, IL: Sourcebooks, Inc. 2006.

Eileen Regan Larence
Prevalence of Domestic Violence, Sexual Assault, Dating Violence, and Stalking, Washington, D.C.: U.S. Government Accountability Office, 2006.

Catherine A. MacKinnon
Women's Lives, Men's Laws, Cambridge, MA: Belknap Press, 2005.

L.Y. Marlow
Color Me Butterfly: A True Story of Courage, Hope, and Transformation, Bowie, MD: eL pub, 2007.

Margie Laird McCue — *A Domestic Violence Handbook, 2nd ed.*, Santa Barbara, CA: ABC-CLIO, 2007.

Lesley McMillan — *Feminists Organizing Against Gendered Violence*, London: Palgrave, 2007.

Linda Mills — *Violent Partners: A Breakthrough Plan for Ending the Cycle of Abuse*, New York: Basic Books, 2008.

Richard B. Pelzer — *A Brother's Journey: Surviving a Childhood of Abuse*, New York: Warner Books, 2005.

Rosalind B. Penfold — *Dragonslippers: This Is What an Abusive Relationship Looks Like*, New York: Black Cat/Grove Press, 2005.

Loraine Radford and Marrianne Hester — *Mothering Through Domestic Violence*, Philadelphia: Jessica Kingsley Publishers, 2006.

Albert R. Roberts — *Battered Women and Their Families: Intervention Strategies and Treatment Programs, Third Edition*, New York: Springer Publishing Company, 2007.

Evan Stark — *Coercive Control: How Men Entrap Women in Personal Life*, New York: Oxford University Press, 2007.

Donald Stewart — *Refuge: A Pathway Out of Domestic Violence and Abuse*, Birmingham, AL: New Hope Publishers, 2004.

Steven Stosny   *You Don't Have to Take It Anymore: Turn Your Resentful, Angry, or Emotionally Abusive Relationship into a Compassionate, Loving One*, New York: Free Press, 2006.

David B. Wexler   *STOP Domestic Violence: Innovative Skills, Techniques, Options and Plans for Better Relationships, 2nd ed.* New York: W.W. Norton & Company, Inc. 2006.

Paula Wilcox   *Surviving Domestic Violence: Gender, Poverty and Agency* New York: Palgrave Macmillan, 2006.

Index